Jeremiah Trist

Historical memoirs of religious dissension

Jeremiah Trist

Historical memoirs of religious dissension

ISBN/EAN: 9783337131708

Printed in Europe, USA, Canada, Australia, Japan

Cover: Foto ©Lupo / pixelio.de

More available books at **www.hansebooks.com**

MEMOIRS

OF

RELIGIOUS DISSENSION;

ADDRESSED TO THE

SEVENTEENTH PARLIAMENT

OF

GREAT BRITAIN.

BY

JEREMIAH TRIST, M.A.

VICAR OF VERYAN, CORNWALL.

SECOND EDITION.

PRO REGE ET GREGE.

LONDON:
PRINTED FOR J. MURRAY, N° 32, FLEET STREET.
M.DCC.XCI.

ADVERTISEMENT.

THE object of the following pages is, to examine and illustrate the principles and actions of the Protestant Dissenters; and to contrast their actual conduct with their professions of attachment to the establishments in church and state. Their determination to persevere in their attacks upon the Test Laws, and the measures which they have adopted in order to secure success in their future application to parliament, appear sufficiently clear from their own deliberate resolutions. " It is our
" earnest wish, that, either in the next session of parli-
" ament, or in the first session after the next general
" election, *every congregation of Protestant Dissenters*
" *throughout the kingdom should, either separately or*
" *jointly, petition the House of Commons for the repeal*
" *of the Test and Corporation Acts.*"

" *We think it desireable that the whole body of Pro-*
" *testant Dissenters should shew a steady regard, at the*
" *ensuing general election, to the support of those can-*
" *didates for seats in parliament, whom they have reason*
" *to believe friendly to the cause of civil and religious*
" *liberty.*"—*See Resolutions of the Meeting of Delegates from eight Congregations of Dissenters, held at Warrington, January 6th,* 1790.

ADVERTISEMENT.

" *It is our earnest wish, that, either in the next session*
" *of parliament, or in the first session after the next*
" *general election, &c.*" as above.—See *Resolutions
of the Meeting of Prot. Diss. held at Bolton, December*
17*th*, 1789.

" *Let it suffice to say, at present, that we are not*
" *discouraged by our late defeat; but shall cherish the*
" *confidence, that, when application for relief from our*
" *grievances is renewed, we shall not be censured as*
" *obstinately persisting in* fruitless attempts. *The time*
" *will speedily arrive, when a generous nation, that of*
" *late has been misled by false alarms, and insidious and*
" *bigotted misrepresentations, shall return to calmer*
" *feelings and more sober reflection. A restoration to*
" *our rights* must *necessarily result from the progress*
" *of truth, justice, and sound policy.*"—See *Address to
the People of England from the Committee of Prot. Diss.
dated London, May* 11*th*, 1790: *Edward Jefferies,
chairman.*

" *Should King, minister, and prelates be arrayed*
" *against them, let not the Protestant Dissenters shrink*
" *from the contest.—Defeated in their first attempts, let*
" *them not abandon their object, but repeat their appli-*
" *cation till the voice of reason shall be heard.* By
" *perseverance they must be victorious.*"—*The
Right of Prot. Diss. &c. asserted, p.* 99.

TO THE

REPRESENTATIVES

OF THE

PEOPLE OF GREAT BRITAIN.

AMONGST the many subjects that may be agitated during the period of your trust, there will be few of greater national importance than the existence of the present Test Laws. The main question relative to their use and design has been intentionally confounded amidst specious arguments for *political freedom*, and claims for *personal merit*. Since their late defeat, it has been contended on the part of the Protestant Dissenters, that the human mind is not yet sufficiently matured by knowledge, or humanized by philosophy; but that the rapid progress of truth, and the true notions of liberty, which begin to possess *the multitude*, are the

seeds

seeds of a salutary revolution, which, being cherished by the culture of a *more indulgent* Parliament, will shortly expand into the perfect bloom of liberty, and overshadow every semblance of ecclesiastical polity and form of worship.

The political services of the Dissenters, likewise, are urged as a subject worthy of your consideration, and as deserving of a just recompence. Their principles and their actions are appealed to as the proper test of their attachment to the civil constitution; and it is in consequence of this position, and in conformity with this favourite doctrine, that the following sheets, which are detached from a larger plan *, are at present submitted to your notice;

---

* It is intended to submit the following subjects to public notice:

1. The harmony of civil and religious polity.
2. The importance of a national church, and the absolute necessity of certain tests to maintain and secure it.
3. The History of the present Test Laws, with every recent objection to them impartially considered.—And a transient view of the Bangorian controversy.
4. Nature and object of free enquiry.

5. Extent

notice; not as comprising the merits of the main question, but as collecting from history and precedent a true and judicious estimate of the real services of the Protestant Dissenters.

It is to the peculiar honour of the late parliament, that it resisted succesfully three several attacks on the established constitution of this country; and it is worthy your observation, that sanguine hopes are cherished by the friends to the repeal of the Test Laws, from what is now termed, the *more enlightened* Members of the present Legislature. But it

5. Extent of abatements and relaxations, in view of promoting uniformity.

6. Ill consequences of the repeal of the present tests, to the state, the clergy, and the public seminaries.

7. Reasons why success cannot attend the petition of the Dissenters.

From this sketch it is obvious, that the subject under discussion, viz. " The actual conduct of the Protestant " Dissenters, contrasted with their professions of attach- " ment to the establishments in church and state," has in its present detached form many unfavourable circumstances to combat; and it would not have been at this time exposed to notice, if it had not a temporary respect, I mean, the determination of the Protestant Dissenters to renew their application to parliament, and their confidence of success with the present legislature.

becomes

becomes you to reflect, that the present Tests were intended, by our experienced ancestors, *to guard against what men may do:* and if, in an evil hour, you should consent to their abrogation, your country is thenceforward reduced to this inevitable destiny, *to trust to what men will do.* A genërous and grateful people has now chearfully extended their confidence to you, implicitly relying on your wisdom, and trusting that their present happy constitution, in church and state, will be maintained pure and undisturbed, and that their best interests will never be betrayed by a vote of the Seventeenth Parliament of Great Britain.

That you may preserve inviolate those sacred rights which have been recently entrusted to you, is the ardent wish of one, who has the *real interests* of Protestant Dissenters much at heart.

August 1st, 1790.

PREFACE.

AN author who undertakes a subject of such latitude and variation as the "Historical Memoirs of religious Dissension," would find it very difficult to execute his design, either for the information of his readers, or the perspicuity of his own ideas, if he did not distribute his subject under certain general heads and divisions. Convinced of the utility of such arrangement, I have adopted a plan, which is to take in the whole merits of the question of late so generally agitated, "The repeal of the Test and Corporation Acts;" a question, which has interest enough in it to awaken the attention of every man who regards the welfare of the community, and the prosperity of the civil and religious establishments.

In the following remarks I may be thought by some to have treated the Protestant Dissenters with too much asperity. To such I beg leave to say, that,

from

from the outset of my enquiry, I have had those only in view, whose political *conduct* has been directly opposite to their *professions* of good-will. The principles of these men, and their attachment to our constitution in church and state, may be very fairly measured by this historical statement of their *actions*. The peaceable citizen, whether a conformist or nonconformist, is equally entitled to attention and respect: on such these strictures cannot fall; for, as they relate little to theological disputes, and are solely intended to discuss the political merits of the Dissenters, they are applicable to those only who disturb the tranquillity of that government, which extends to all its members the blessings of civil and religious liberty.

I am as sensible as any man, that there are, amongst the Protestant Dissenters, men truly eminent for piety, virtue, and moderation. Far be it that a tittle of censure should fall on such: indeed there cannot, in the present instance; for, as they do not stand accused, no imputation of faction, or of insincerity, will attach to them. But should the peaceable and moderate Dissenter feel some smart, some compunction, from these remarks, it must be attributed either to the misconduct of his distempered brethren, or to his having, in some remote degree, connected himself with them in their late injudicious measures. In either case, I am to be

acquitted

acquitted of detraction, but muſt remind this reſpectable citizen, that

" The mildew'd ear may blaſt his wholeſome brother."
Shak.

Having premiſed thus much, it may be proper to aſſign ſome reaſon for my preſent appearance at the tribunal of the public. I have witneſſed, in common with others, the late diſturbance of the public tranquillity, under the ſpecious pretext of obtaining an extenſion of civil and religious liberty. I have ſeen too, with concern, that the abettors of the propoſed reformation are firmly reſolved to perſevere in their attempts to aboliſh thoſe fences of the conſtitution, which the common anceſtor has eſtabliſhed: and, as I am as nearly concerned in the maintenance and ſupport of them, as the Diſſenters may be in their demolition, I have taken ſome pains to enquire into the merit of their preſent enterprize, and the reach of thoſe arguments upon which they found their claim. My preſent object, then, is to clear their ſpecious arguments from that fallacy and ſophiſtication in which they are enveloped, and not to widen a breach already too expoſed, by entering into theological controverſy.

I have only to requeſt my reader, not to impute any intemperance, which he may fancy he diſcovers in the following pages, to a want of candour or of good-will for the Diffenters, as fuch, but to that difguft which is natural to every man who fees religion, the chief band of fociety, made a ftalking-horfe to difturb that tranquillity which we *may* all enjoy under an adminiftration fo mild and equal as the prefent.

My fentiments upon a difference in religious opinions, as affecting the public peace, and my abhorrence of perfecution for confcience fake, I fhall leave with my reader in the words of an illuftrious ftatefman and confummate politician.

" Of this I may give only this advice, according
" to my fmall model:—Men ought to take heed of
" rending God's church by two kinds of contro-
" verfies: The one is, when the matter of the point
" controverted is too fmall and light, not worth the
" heat and ftrife about it, kindled only by contra-
" diction. For, as it is noted by one of the fathers,
" *Chrift's coat indeed had no feam; but the churches*
" *vefture was of divers colours:*" whereupon he
" faith, " *In vefte varietas fit, fciffura non fit;*"
" they be two things, unity and uniformity.—The
" other is, when the matter of the point contro-
" verted is great, but it is driven to an over-great
" fubtilty and obfcurity, fo that it becometh a thing
" rather ingenious than fubftantial. A man that is
" of judgment and underftanding, fhall fometimes
" hear ignorant men differ, and know well within
" himfelf,

PREFACE.

"himself, that those which so differ mean one
"thing, and yet they themselves would never
"agree. And if it come so to pass, in that distance
"of judgment which is between man and man,
"shall we not think, that God above, that knows
"the heart, doth not discern that frail men in some
"of their contradictions intend the same thing, and
"accepteth of both? The nature of such contro-
"versies is excellently expressed by St. Paul, in
"the warning and precept that he giveth concern-
"ing the same, * *Devita profanas vocum novitates, et
"oppositiones falsi nominis scientiæ.* Men create op-
"positions which are not, and put them into new
"terms so fixed, as whereas the meaning ought
"to govern the term, the term in effect governeth
"the meaning.—Concerning *the means of procuring
"unity*; men must beware, that in the procuring
"or muniting of religious unity, they do not dis-
"solve, and deface the laws of charity, and of hu-
"man society. There are two swords amongst
"Christians, the spiritual and temporal; and *both
"have their due office and place in the maintenance of
"religion.* But we may not take up the third
"sword, which is Mahomet's sword, or like unto
"it: that is, to propagate religion by wars, or by
"sanguinary persecutions to force consciences, ex-

* " Avoid profane and vain babblings, and oppositions of
" science falsely so called." 1 Tim. vi. 20.

" cept

"cept it be in cases of overt-scandal, blasphemy, or intermixture of practice against the state: *much less to nourish seditions, to authorize conspiracies and rebellions, to put the sword into the people's hands,* and the like, tending to the subversion of all government, which is the ordinance of God. For this is but to dash the first table against the second, and so to consider men as Christians, as we forget that they are men."—Sir F. Bacon's Essays.

ERRATA.

Page 9. Note, line 10. *for* inferences, *read* inference.
—— 24. Note, line 1. *for* brother electors, *read* readers.

HISTORICAL MEMOIRS

OF

RELIGIOUS DISSENSION.

THE friends and advocates for the repeal of the Test and Corporation Acts have been forward in celebrating the exploits and atchievements of the Dissenters, as one popular argument in support of their cause. They have represented them as the chief authors and restorers of civil and religious liberty, as foremost in promoting schemes of public utility, intelligent in planning, active and intrepid in conducting them, and, in fact, as the props and pillars of the present constitution in church and state. Had their pamphlets and declamations rested here, the fond panegyric would not, in all probability, have been disturbed, or excited attention and inquiry. But, in order to heighten the encomium, and perfect the illusion, they have unmercifully dragged the clergy of the establishment into an unhappy contrast, and, to magnify the merits of their compeers, they have overwhelmed this unfortunate description of men with obloquy and derision.

Thus, to dignify the offices, and elevate the reputation of the dissenting ministry, we are told, "*That the episcopal character is degraded by modern prelates, and the most sacred ceremonies prostituted to state policy and persecution* *." To promote the temporal interests of nonconformity, we are apprized, "*That the chief obstacles to religious liberty lie in the bigotry and habitual bad politics of established churchmen, and in the complaisance of timid or subtle statesmen in their favour* †." To obviate any conceit of liberal and enlightened times, we are reminded, "*That the age in which we live is unfavourable to religious freedom, that an inquiry into truth is checked by the civil powers, and the spread of genuine Christianity chilled by the cold influence of splendid establishments* ‡." And, to complete the measure of their ignominy, we are assured, "*That churchmen are unfriendly to the house of Brunswick, infringers on the rights of mankind, oppressors, and persecutors* ‖."

It

---

* Right of the Protestant Dissenters to a complete Toleration asserted. p. 96, & seq.—Advertisement to the Life of Monf. Claude, by R. Robinson of Cambridge.

† New and old Principles of Trade compared, p. 50.

‡ Priestley' Importance of free Inquiry.

‖ Priestley's Letter to the Rt. Hon. Wm. Pitt.—Censures of the same complexion were pretty strongly implied in the speeches of the Rt. Hon. Ch. J. Fox, and Henry Beaufoy, esq; in the house of commons, March 3d, 1790, on the motion, That the house resolve

It muſt be acknowledged that the reſolutions of the Proteſtant Diſſenters, in their late meetings *, convey more favourable impreſſions; their language is, in general, conciliating, and their profeſſions of attachment and good-will forcibly arreſt the judgment, and calm thoſe diſingenuous emotions ſo natural in contending intereſts. The mild expoſtulations of thoſe who are ſtruggling with oppreſſion, and who are pleading for a redreſs of grievances, under the perſuaſion of general harmony, and the welfare of all diſtinctions, ſpeak feelingly to the heart, and tempt us to accuſe ourſelves of partiality and want of candour for withholding implicit confidence in ſuch fair profeſſions. For my own part, as I cannot give chearful credence to theſe declarations, it is but honeſt that I ſhould aſſign my reaſons: I ſuſpect treachery ſomewhere, and, if their reſolutions are not maſked, why have not the Diſſenters muzzled their loud apologiſts?—To do juſtice to a cauſe of ſome moment, I have taken pains to examine the fair pages of hiſtory, to which they ſo frequently refer us; but from hence I have drawn intelligence not at all favourable to their ſincerity; and I have no ſcruple in ſaying, that it will require the abilities of

reſolve itſelf into a Committee on the ſubject of the Teſt Acts.

* Towards the cloſe of the year 1789, and in the beginning of 1790, the ſectaries of different denominations, aſſuming the common title of Proteſtant Diſſenters, convened public meetings throughout moſt of the counties, and many principal towns of the kingdom.

a very able casuist to reconcile these public declarations of good-will to the present establishment with the actual conduct of the leading characters amongst the Protestant Dissenters.

To examine their proceedings with that impartiality which is due to a respectable class of men, and that perspicuity so necessary in a contest where much misrepresentation may be expected on both sides, I am tempted to consider them under two distinctions, that I may not at large impute dissimulation and inconsistency to such a numerous body of citizens, many of whom are no doubt men of high integrity and worth. In the following discussion I would distinguish the *moderate dissenter* from the restless and zealous reformer. The object of the *first*, as far as he is concerned in the plan of innovation, is to soften those obstructions which have hitherto interposed betwixt him and the Establishment, to which he approaches, with a view to union, as near as he conscientiously can; of *the second*, to pull down the national church, and to erect some hitherto-undefined and visionary fabric in its room. *The moderate dissenter*, not unmindful of the importance of church communion, and the harmony of civil and religious polity, labours for reconciliation, upon the principles of improving the reformation, and of purifying and perfecting the protestant cause; whilst the *disturbed votary*, eager to express his abhorrence of rites and ceremonies, of liturgies and hierarchies, sinks his patriotism in his zeal, and, like the overheated bigot of the sixteenth century,

century, betrays only his wish, "*to have one pluck more at the whore of Babylon's red petticoat.*" From the furious assaults of the last, the constitution has not much to dread; but upon a union of these formidable powers, the best-constituted state has reason to be upon its guard; for when political jealousy is lulled into an imaginary security by the fair language of calm expostulation, the state is, in fact, more exposed to the furious attacks of fanaticism and disaffection.

I would not, therefore, be understood to charge every dissenter, who has attached himself to this general confederacy, with dissimulation, or with views injurious to the public safety; yet, as they have thought proper to associate themselves under one general denomination *, the peaceable dissenter, as far as he has joined interests with the factious separatist, must be exposed to that scrutiny and censure which may fall upon the latter, since he is in fact responsible for the excesses of his less temperate

---

* There is no small address in comprising the various sectaries under one general denomination of Protestant Dissenter; under this ambiguous term the advocates for dissension appeal to history, under the cloak of Presbyterianism, for instances of conformity and rigid attachment to establishments, and, as occasion may serve, they shift to Independency in proof of their maintenance of religious freedom and liberty of conscience. The answering such immethodical writers may be compared to the diversion of *hunting the duck*, in the words of Monsieur Bayle; " When I have him in full view, and fancy him within my " reach, he slips from me, takes a dip, and becomes invisi- " ble."

associate, agreeable to that just maxim of the elegant Tibullus,

"Quicquid agit, sanguis est tamen illa tuus."

To the professions of the first, great attention is due; to the influence of these men I attribute that moderation in which their printed resolutions are in general couched. It is impossible to withhold one's approbation of the temper and disinterestedness of the following resolutions: "That, "with respect to the use of fair reasoning and ar- "gument, the repeal of the Acts in question will "give us no advantage which we do not already "possess; and that we explicitly disavow, as a "body, every act of intemperate zeal, and declare, "that we will not give our sanction or support to "the indiscreet warmth of any individual *." Their open contempt of private interest claims also no small notice: "While we thus assert our rights "to all the privileges of good citizens, we publicly "disclaim all pretensions to the dignities and emo- "luments which are by law attached to the esta- "blished church," &c †.

And, in proof of their sincerity, they refer us to their uniform good conduct throughout the last century: "We appeal to the uniform conduct of all "denominations among us, for the space of a whole "century, and particularly in two critical periods, "when there was not a single Protestant Dissenter "who joined the hostile banners of a pretender to

* Resolution of the Meeting of Protestant Dissenters of the riding of York, held at Wakefield, December 30, 1789.
† Id.

"the

" the throne, or was suspected of an attachment to
" his cause *."

Such temperate and ingenuous language, whether under real or imaginary oppression, demands attention; and if it should be found, upon examination, to contain neither artifice nor sophistry, who would refuse unfeigned credit to such friendly declarations? But, to examine into their declared uniformity of attachment to the constitution of this country, I must be permitted to go a little further back into history than that period whence the Protestant Dissenters have thought proper to date their loyalty and good-will: this, indeed, is a justice due to their cause, since it will be a brief chronicle of the times when they were in power, and when under real persecution.

To trace the progress of religious dissension through the dark periods immediately succeeding the reformation, would be a tedious and uninteresting task; I shall therefore briefly observe, that although much greater reasons prevailed at that time, than there do at present, for separation, yet there was no disagreement about the terms of church communion: Hooper, Ridley, Rogers, and others, the then controversialists, were reconciled to each other; and it may be fairly presumed that Ridley, Cranmer, and Latimer, who laid down their lives for the Establishment, had searched as narrowly into the abuses of the reformed church as any

---

* Resolution of the Wakefield Meeting.

amongſt the preſent diſſenters. There was in this period no ſeparate meetings, except of ſome of the more furious anabaptiſts and ſecret papiſts, as is implied in biſhop Ridley's Articles of Viſitation, 1550 *. But the moderation of the firſt reformers, in regard to church ceremonies and eſtabliſhments, was ſuch that we find Calvin, Beza †, Peter Martyr, &c. men whoſe zeal in many reſpects carried them to great lengths, uniting upon the broad principles of reconciliation, commending uniformity, and expoſing the danger of contending for a few ceremonies, "*whether ſuch as were appointed for decency, or thoſe that were ſymbolical* ‡."

If it ſhould be ſaid, that in thoſe days the danger from the church of Rome was more imminent, and that on this account the firſt reformers were leſs vigilant, leſt by needleſs ſcrupuloſity they ſhould check the progreſs of reformation, I have this to urge, that the dread of popery was not only then, but has been ever ſince, the chief foundation of diſſenting patriotiſm.

I ſhall paſs over the ſhort reign of unrelenting Mary, as little applicable to the preſent ſubject. Upon the acceſſion of Elizabeth, and the reſtoration

---

* Sparrow's Canons, p. 35, 4to edit.—Stillingfleet on Separation, part i. ſect. 5.

† Beza defines the ſin of Separation to conſiſt, "not merely "in going from one church to another, but the diſcontinuing "communion with the public aſſemblies, as though one were no "member of them." Epiſt. 24. p. 148.

‡ Calvin's Epiſtle to Sadolet, de vera Reformatione.

of the church, the Jesuitical party began to sow the seeds of division; to check the growth of which, and of a disaffection to the state which now began to manifest itself amongst the non-conformists, the act of Uniformity came forth, expressly against the Dissenters *. An open separation had now taken place, as Camden informs us, " under pretence of " a purer reformation, by opposition to the disci- " pline, liturgy, and calling of our bishops, as ap- " proaching too near to the church of Rome †."

From hence then we must date that dissension which has since raged with such indecent violence ‡.

* In 1559, anno primo Elizabethæ.

† Annales Elizabethæ, an. dom. 1568.—This circumstance is misstated by a very shrewd writer, who professes to give an *impartial* history of the Tests, which, as he thinks, has never before been *fairly given*. This advocate says, " The Sacra- " ment of the Lord's Supper had been made a test of the prin- " ciples of the communicant here, prior to the year 1571, *which* " *was long before any Protestants had openly separated from the Es-* " *tablishment.*" Right of Prot. Diff. asserted, Pref. & p. 1.— If this writer could establish his facts, his inferences might be fair enough, That, as the Tests existed before separation, they could not have been designed against Protestant Dissenters.

‡ In 1568. See Stillingfleet on Separation, part i. sect. 6 & 7.—*The notable Assertor* of the Rights of the Protestant Dissenters affirms, " That Bishop Stillingfleet dates the entire separation " of the Dissenters from the Church from the time of the " King's declaration of indulgence, issued in the year 1671-2." Such inaccuracies are so very frequent with this writer, that they would be overlooked, if he did not deduce his sophistical inferences from them. See Rights of Prot. Diff. asserted, p. 4.

It

It has frequently been obferved, that, in proportion to the profperity of this country, and its fecurity from foreign hoftilities, religious faction has been feen to flourifh. Thus, under the firm and fuccefsful reign of Elizabeth, thefe holy feuds kept pace with its encreafing power, and in a very few years we find a formidable party fetting up a feparate worfhip in oppofition to the eftablifhed church: whereas, under the feeble government of the latter Stuarts, in particular, when there were continual apprehenfions of papal power, faction forgat its nature, and fchifmatics crowded into fubjection, to oppofe the inroads of tyranny and intolerance.

Thefe early diffenters, under pretence of more evangelical purity, refifted the ceremonies, habit, and doctrine of the national religion, and in a fhort time grew fo troublefome to the ftate, by attempting to confine the Queen's fupremacy to a temporal jurifdiction, and by publicly refufing to attend the divine fervice of the church, that Elizabeth, in addition to the Act of Uniformity, thought it fafe, in the year 1569, and again * in 1571, to publifh proclamations, enforcing uniformity, and a due attendance on the facraments, under heavy penalties, *as a teft of the allegiance of her fubjects*; in confequence of which, the laws againft the non-conformifts were put in force, and feveral of the principal diffenters were fufpended, deprived, and imprifoned.

* See Sparrow's Canons.

prifoned *. I do not mean to juftify thefe harſh proceedings againſt the feparatifts, or the real perfecution which in fome inſtances difgraced this reign †. I only notice thefe feverities, in order to controvert thofe unqualified aſſertions, which the apologifts for diſſenſion make, " That the tefts " were enacted previous to feparation, and uni- " formly levelled againſt the papifts;" whereas the direct contrary is the fact, they originated in feparation, and were defigned as a teft of the principles and allegiance of the non-conformifts.

But what puts this matter beyond a queſtion, is, that at the time we are treating of, when the act of Uniformity paſſed, and the Sacramental Teft was firſt enforced, the Papifts were more peaceable fubjects, more in favour with the queen, and freer

---

* The advocates for the diſſenters roundly aſſert " That " there was no poſitive law or injunction for perfons to receive " the facrament of the Lord's fupper, until the popiſh plot had " put the nation in a ferment, when the ſtatute of the 3d of " James I. was enacted, 1606." Right of Pr. Diſſ. p. 2d.— Thefe writers artfully pafs over the act of uniformity, and the book of common prayer fet forth by the common confent of the realm, and by *authority of parliament*, in the firſt year of Elizabeth, and likewife her proclamation fourteen years after (viz. 1573) enjoining the magiftrate, " to fearch after and *puniſh* all " fuch perfons as ſhall forbear to come to the common prayer, " *and receive the facraments of the church*, according to the order " in the faid book," &c. Sparrow's canons.—This was purpofely levelled at the fectaries, and not againſt the *papiſts*.

† In the latter part of this reign thefe fanguinary laws againſt the diſſenters, which were a difgrace to Chriftianity, were, for reafons of ſtate, judged proper to be repealed.

from

from persecution, than the Protestant Dissenters were: for it was not till that haughty prelate Pius V. fulminated his bull against Elizabeth, in 1569, that she thought the popish a formidable party; whereas the sectaries, by their turbulence and disaffection to the established church, threatened her supremacy, and the interruption of the public safety. It appears too, that at an examination taken before Grindal, bishop of London, 20th June, 1567, several persons were accused not only of absenting themselves from their parish churches, " but of gathering together, making assemblies, " using prayers and preachings, *and ministring sa-* " *craments amongst themselves.*" This occasioned the act of uniformity to be pressed with some rigour, yet not more than was necessary; for Gilby, *himself a dissenter*, insinuates, " That if they had been let " alone a little longer, they would have shaken the " constitution of the church *."

The apprehensions of James I. from the Protestant Dissenters appears by his attempts to reconcile them to the establishment soon after he ascended the throne: but the conference held at Hampton Court for this purpose, failing of its desired effect, the Dissenters were exposed to the severities of the canons established in 1603; a heavy blow upon the Papists, as well as the Dissenters from the established church, many of whom suffered at the stake for their disaffection, through the horrible policy of this feeble administration.

* See Stillingfleet on Separation, p. 20.

The

The reign of Charles I. presents us with episcopacy in all its splendor; the Puritans, to whom Charles seemed at first attached, began soon to take offence at the fabulous innovations * of some of the prelacy; and, as the Presbyterian worship had been already declared to have no foundation in scripture, nor in the practice of the church, these offended sects joined with the Independents, ever averse to ecclesiastical establishments, and overthrew the discipline of the church, dethroning that unhappy monarch, whose over-weening attachment to the hierarchy was a principal cause of civil discord, and hastened the ruin of the constitution. Hitherto we have seen little affection on the part of the Dissenters, either for monarchy, or the national church, but an invariable deviation from that wholesome advice of the old † non-conformists,

---

* Particularly some ill-founded reports of archbishop Laud.

† Baxter, an eminent dissenter, in his Defence of the Cure of Divisions, expresses himself in the following ingenuous terms: "The most learned and worthy of the old non-conformists, wrote more against separation, than the conformists: and the present non-conformists have not more wisdom, learning, or holiness than they: but they did not only urge the people against separation, but to come to the very beginning of the public worship, preferring it before their private duties." p. 88. &c.—See also on this subject Beza's 23d epistle to bishop Grindal, Gualter's epistle to Cox, bishop of Ely, and Zanchius's epistle to bishop Jewel.—I must subjoin here the opinion of John Fox, a rational non-conformist. This honest and sensible man, apprehensive of the ill consequences of that turbulent and factious spirit which had got amongst his dissenting brethren, complains, "That

mists, for a chearful compliance and reconciliation to the legal establishments.

We are now presented with Dissension first in power; how it availed itself may be collected, with sufficient censure, from writers at all times favourable to it. As soon as the Presbyterians had got the upper hand, we find them peremptorily refusing that indulgence to others, which, during the episcopacy, they had so unceasingly pleaded for themselves, even to those very men, who, by joining with them in the overthrow of the constitution, had compassed their establishment. And so rigid were they in point of uniformity, that they even complained of a want of church power sufficient to crush *the sectaries*, as they could now call all those who differed from them: to such a degree of rigour did they proceed, that, by a memorable ordinance in 1645, the use of the common prayer book was prohibited, not only in public worship but in private families, under heavy penal-

" That some of his party began to despise him, because he
" could not rail against bishops and archbishops as they did;
" but, if he could be as mad as they, they would be kinder to
" him. And therefore he soberly adviseth the governors of the
" church to look well after this sort of men; for if they prevail,
" it is not to be imagined what mischief and disturbance they
" will bring; whose hypocrisy is more subtle and pernicious
" than that of the old monks; for, under pretence of greater
" purity, they will never give over, till they have brought men
" under a Jewish slavery." See Fuller's Church History, l. 9.
p. 306.—Such were the sentiments of a rational dissenter in the last century.

ties;

ties; and a fine of 50*l.* was incurred by any person, who should preach, write, or print any thing in derogation of the Directory of the presbyterian worship. One instance of intolerance cannot be overlooked in this place, an instance that baffles comparison in the darkest ages of unrelenting bigotry: these *vindicators of liberty and the rights* of man refused to indulge their oppressed monarch with the chiefest consolation to insulted feelings, and a broken spirit, positively stipulating, in the treaty of the Isle of Wight, that the king should not be allowed the indulgence of a common prayer book for the private use of himself and family. Till this revolution the real principles of Dissenters were never known; they had been heretofore claiming indulgence from those that were in power, but now, being vested with authority, they became the bitter persecutors of their rivals; and the advocates for freedom of conscience, and the natural rights of mankind, were now transformed into furious bigots, and the engines of intolerance;

> " And man, proud man,
> " Drest in a little brief authority,
> " Play'd such fantastic tricks before high Heaven,
> " As made the angels weep."
> MEAS. FOR MEAS.

Perhaps, if I was to question a dissenter of the present day on such unexampled persecution, he might tell me that this was the act of the Presbyterian, or of the Independent, or of the Anabaptist.

Vain

Vain effort at exculpation! Fruitless attempt to limit the operation of intolerance!—But how must his ingenuity be put to the test to parry a narrative of complicated oppression! The unfortunate Mr. John Biddle, a writer of some eminence amongst the Socinians, experienced, in this *æra of liberty*, the singular fate of having an *Anabaptist* for his accuser, a *Presbyterian* for his judge, and an *Independent* to execute his sentence. By the former, Griffin, an Anabaptist teacher, who had challenged him to a public disputation, he was betrayed, in the course of the controversy, to " deny that Christ was God:" his illiterate opponent, unable to refute the Socinian, accused him of blasphemy, and procured an order for his commitment to Newgate; in consequence of which he was tried for his life, but his sentence was changed by Cromwell, for banishment into the islands of Scilly *.

I shall be excused inserting in this place the judicious remarks upon these times of an elegant and enlightened writer †, and the rather because he was not a member of an episcopal church. " These
" broils and tumults served also unhappily to con-
" firm the truth of an observation often made,
" that all religious sects, while they are kept un-
" der and oppressed, are remarkable for inculcat-
" ing the duties of moderation, forbearance, and

---

* In 1655.—See short account of the life of T. Biddle, prefixed to 1st vol. of Society Tracts, 1691.

† Mosheim's Ecclesiastical History, translated by Dr. Maclaine, vol. iv. p. 522.

" charity

"charity towards those who dissent from them: but as soon as the scenes of persecution are removed, and they, in their turn, arrive at power and pre-eminence, they forget their own precepts and maxims, and leave both the recommendation and practice of charity to those that groan under their yoke. Such, in reality, was the conduct and behaviour of the Puritans, during their transitory exaltation; they shewed as little clemency and equity to the bishops, and other patrons of episcopacy, as they had received from them when the reins of government were in their hands."

But let us turn from this degrading picture of human nature, to that period where the dissenters challenge our admiration, bidding us recollect that to them we owe the restoration of the monarchy, and the re-establishment of the church*.

Able

---

* " The aid of the dissenters has more than once been wanted, to secure the civil liberties of this country, and even to befriend the ecclesiastical establishments of it, and it may be wanted again. Our ancestors were instrumental both in the restoration of the Stuarts, and in the settlement of the crown upon the present family." Priestley's letter to the Right Hon. William Pitt, p. 51.

" Trusting to Charles II's declaration from Breda, the presbyterians, notwithstanding a strong opposition from the other sects, entered heartily into his views, and compassed his restoration.—By means of the restoration, the church of England was tacitly re-established." See Rights of the Protestant Dissenters asserted, p. 5.

Able panegyrists of faction and sedition! Let us examine a little into this sudden change from rebellion to allegiance, from persecution to protection. The facts, as recorded by the best historians, stand thus:—The presbyterians, dissatisfied that their church, although now become the national establishment, did not empower them sufficiently to compel rigid uniformity, were continually harrassing the parliament for more coercive powers, in order to prosecute all those who differed from them in religious opinions: upon this the army, consisting chiefly of independents, with independent Cromwell at their head, were violently incensed against them, and betook itself to the desperate measure of assuming the sovereign power, and at last became so far masters as to hold the presbyterians in a sort of subjection. These, finding the tables now turned upon them, and that in fact they had no longer any thing more than the shadow of authority in the state, and being now thoroughly sensible that their

---

The roman catholic claims equal notice, as the framer of the British constitution, and the improver of civil government: the present titular bishop of London, in one of his many ingenious publications, pleads with like dexterity. " In the various " abuse that has been thrown out on catholics, it seems " never to occur to any one, that many valuable parts of the " English constitution were framed by them.—Shall the English " catholics, then, who reared this constitution, at the great ex-" pence of their lives and fortunes, and who loved it in its un-" finished state, shall they hate and attempt its ruin, when it " has acquired due form and stability?" See Berrington on the Rights of the Dissenters.

lot was even more severe than under monarchy, and the national church, began to think of restoring Charles II. to the throne; accordingly, upon his artful declaration from Breda, they joined the episcopalians, and thus assisted in the restoration of the monarchy, and re-establishment of the church of England.

Such then were the tender mercies of presbyterianism! and such the real motives of their boasted services and attachment to the constitution!

> "So fellest foes,
> "Whose passions, and whose plots have broke their sleep,
> "To take the one the other, by some chance,
> "Some trick not worth an egg, shall grow dear friends,
> "And interjoin their issues,"   CORIOLANUS.

The aim of Charles II. to restore popery was soon suspected by the dissenters, and perhaps nothing manifested his intentions more than his declaration for toleration in 1672, which suspended all the penal laws both against papists and dissenters; and we find the latter quietly acquiescing under the famous test act which passed in the following year, as more consonant to their wishes, than the former clemency of their king, at the bottom of which they saw both popery and slavery. The reigns of the latter Stuarts, in particular, present us, at every juncture, with the jealousies and apprehensions of the non-conformists, lest the revival of popery should deprive them, in common with the members of the establishment, of their religious privileges, and involve them in calamities more severe than churchmen would be exposed to; who, according to their own accounts, retaining much of *the old leaven of antichrist*, would consequently experience fewer restrictions *. The attachment then of the dissenters to the establishment, during this period, though not very conspicuous, must be attributed to this cause—the mutual interests of both parties were concerned in one common opposition to popery, which was ever on the watch, waiting secretly for an opportunity to restore persecution and intolerance.

The house of Stuart, through a series of selfish policy, began now to totter; and a continuance of indiscreet and ruinous measures, during the short reign of inglorious James, completed its destruction. We are presented in this reign with a singular phenomenon, *a popish king a strenuous advocate for universal toleration* †. " Strange doctrine," says Burnet, " in
" the

---

* Some dissenters of the present times affirm that the reformation has not completely thrown down the kingdom of antichrist, who still retains dominion over the British establishment. See Richards's free thoughts on the corruptions of Christianity, 1784.

† So *tolerant* was James at this time, that he granted permission to the lord mayor of London, a presbyterian, to use what form of worship he liked best in Guildhall chapel: but the wary dissenter, *being a friend to the establishment*, refused the generous offer: in other words, he saw through the artful design, to engage him to make the first change from the established worship, and that if a presbyterian minister officiated this year, no doubt a popish

" the mouth of a profeffed papift;" and which is only thus to be accounted for:—The clergy of the eftablifhment having oppofed the artful defigns of the court to revive popery, were difgraced, and the diffenters in their turn taken into high favour; thefe bore their exaltation unbecomingly: but the moft moderate amongft them, (and there have been moderate diffenters in all ages) reftrained in fome degree the infolence of the reft; they faw that this brightnefs of royal favour was only a fun-beam, and a defign of the papifts, to create an open breach betwixt them and the church party*.

But I haften to that fecond grand crifis of patriotifm, to which the proteftant diffenters refer us, as a proof of their being *the friends to ecclefiaftical eftablifhments, and the reftorers of civil liberty.* There is one memorable inftance in which their *attachment* to the eftablifhment, and their *zeal for civil liberty*, was not altogether fo confpicuous. Although I cannot pafs it over in filence, becaufe it greatly haftened that glorious revolution, which, as they juftly obferve, they did promote; yet I fhall be fo impartial as to let their favourite hiftorian † relate the circumftance. " Towards the end of April 1688,
" the

pifh prieft would have celebrated mafs there in the next. And the cautious magiftrate, under the wifdom of the ferpent, affumed the harmleffnefs of the dove.

* See Burnet's Hiftory of his Own Times, an. 1686.

† The diffenters are fond of referring to Dr. Burnet, as an hiftorian very favourable to their caufe, and a declared foe to the clergy; the good bifhop, with much candour, however, cautions them not to rely too implicitly on his reprefentations.

"the king thought fit to renew the declaration,
"that he had set out the former year, for liberty of
"conscience. Not satisfied with the publishing his
"declaration, he resolved to oblige the clergy to
"read it in all their churches in the time of divine
"service. This put the clergy under great diffi-
"culties, and they were at first much divided
"about it. The point at present was not, whether
"a toleration was a lawful or an expedient thing.
"The declaration was founded on the claim of
"*a dispensing power*, which the king did now af-
"sume, that tended to the total subversion of the
"government, and the making it arbitrary: whereas
"by the constitution it was a legal administration.
"It also allowed such infinite liberty, with the sus-
"pension of all penal laws, and that without any
"limitation, that paganism itself might be now pub-
"licly professed. It was visible, that the design, in
"imposing the reading it on the clergy, was only
"to make them ridiculous, and to make them
"contribute to their own ruin." Thus far Burnet;
who, after commenting on the indecent heats
of the dissenters against the clergy, now become,
by their manly resistance of despotism, exceed-
ingly obnoxious to the court, proceeds to relate,
that it was by the *express advice of the dissenters*,
now in the fulness of royal favour, that James
was induced to commit to the Tower the six

"The peevishness, the ill nature, and the ambition of many
"clergymen, has sharpened my spirits perhaps too much against
"them: so I warn my reader to take all that I say on these
"heads with some grains of allowance." Preface to the History
of his Own Times.

bishops,

bishops, who, in defence of the constitution, positively refused to read the declaration, and resisted this daring attempt at arbitrary power.

The abettors of this notorious transaction have then, in truth, the merit of greatly promoting that glorious revolution, which a few months afterwards was actually completed, by the expulsion of an infatuated bigot from the throne, and the re-establishment of the constitution.

This short view of the conduct of the protestant dissenters for near a century and half, presents us with the sad effects of religious faction; we see the peace of the community perpetually interrupted, civil liberty trampled upon, and the constitution actually overturned in the tumultuous struggles for religious rights and ecclesiastical pre-eminence. That the ancestors of the protestant dissenters were the *unprovoked* authors of these convulsions, I would by no means be understood to insinuate; the persecutions which their discontents and remonstrances had so frequently brought upon them, and those severe penal statutes which the government from time to time judged necessary, to curb the feuds of its domestic enemies, and to preserve the public peace, had now encroached largely on the liberties of the subject, and reduced the privileges of the non-conformists below the condition of free citizens: and, although they occasionally enjoyed some transient gleams of indulgence, through the varying spirit of the court and ministry, yet their situation was always precarious, and they were never entirely free

from fears and perplexities; we are not then to wonder at their restlessness, and frequent attempts to subvert the government, since it was the only chance they had of gaining the upper hand, and of securing to themselves that liberty, which this memorable revolution has so effectually established. We are rather to wonder at that paradox in politics, in which the present advocates of the dissenters have involved their cause, who, whilst they are challenging, in behalf of their forefathers, an eminent share of merit in constructing that beautiful fabric, the present constitution, are equally lavish in their applauses of the descendant for his pious attempts to deface the noblest monument of his ancestor's wisdom. This, however, may be easily reconciled, upon the argument of a Roman author:—" *Dissen-*
" *tientium* res gestæ, sicut ego existumo, satis
" amplæ, verum aliquanto minores tamen, quam
" famâ feruntur: sed, quia provenere ibi magna
" scriptorum ingenia, per terrarum orbem facta
" pro maximis celebrantur. *Ita eorum, qui ea*
" *fecere, virtus tanta habetur, quantum verbis ea po-*
" *tuere extollere præclara ingenia* *."

Upon

---

* For the sake of my brother electors, who may have forgotten their Latin, or never learnt it, I will translate the passage, apprizing them that I have substituted the first word for *Atheniensium*, which I find in the original, vid. Sallust, Bell. Catil. 8. " As
" far as I can judge, fame speaks higher of their atchieve-
" ments, great as they may be, than she ought to do; this may
" be owing to the great ingenuity of their historians and pane-
" gyrists, who have extolled their exploits to the very skies. It
" has

Upon the re-establishment of the constitution, the dissenters came in for that share of religious liberty, to which, as a free people, they were entitled. And the act of toleration, by delivering them from those penal laws which had endangered their persons and property, restored them to that rank in the political scale, which was judged expedient, and safe to the constitution. They are well warranted then in paying a just tribute of applause and gratitude to the common ancestor, whose wisdom and virtue effected the glorious revolution, that epocha of true English liberty. The blind and implicit submission of James to the papal see, which was on the point of re-assuming its tyranny

---

" has so happened then that the reputation of the dissenters, has
" risen in proportion to the wit and abilities of their apologists."
—Mr. Beaufoy, in his very able support of Mr. Fox's motion towards the repeal of the Tests, March 3d, 1790, observed that the conduct of the Protestant Dissenters had been exemplarily peaceable and modest; that in the unhappy moments of national embarrassment, they have preferred a continuance of suffering to every hope of relief; that it was not till all public difficulties and anxieties were removed, that it was not till the return of the general strength, that they have entreated the attention of the legislature to the hardships they have endured from the sacramental tests; and such has been the continuance of their conduct for *more than* 120 *years!*—Credat Judæus.

WOODFALL's DIARY.

And Sir Henry Hoghton at the same time declared, that, as a Protestant Dissenter, he looked with pride to the history of the times *preceding* the passing of these acts.—Thus do these gentlemen, betwixt them, vindicate the *whole political conduct* of the Dissenters, from the date of separation (1559, or according to Camden 1563) to the present times.

over

over civil and religious liberty, had brought the protestant cause to the brink of ruin, and arbitrary power had nearly annihilated the rights and privileges of the subject. But the complaints of an oppressed people increasing with the injuries that were accumulating on them, the season was come when resistance was not only justifiable, but a virtue: the arbitrary monarch fled from his throne, the long-contested limits of royal prerogative were defined, and the sacred and inviolable rights of the subject ascertained.

The mutual jealousies that subsisted betwixt William and a great part of his clergy was not a little fomented by the dissenters, immediately after the prince of Orange was called to the throne. The king, who had a natural bias to Calvinism, and who yielded to no prince in political abilities, had an early opportunity of shewing his aversion to the members of the church of England, and especially the bishops, many of whom, by their refusal to take the oaths of allegiance, and by withdrawing from his parliament, openly disowned his authority and avowed their contempt of his government. To mortify these men, whose strong prejudices in favour of the late doctrine of passive obedience and non-resistance, and whose notions of hereditary, indefeasible right, and direct lineal succession, could not be got over, William resolved to admit the dissenters to a share in posts under the government. To this end, as a previous step, he proposed to parliament the abolition of the Tests; a measure
which,

which, in the former reign, he could by no means be brought to countenance, and which, in all probability, would not have been even now brought forward, but with a view to humble the high nonjuring clergy. The attempt, however, after repeated trials, failed; yet the conteſt was eventually productive of the beſt conſequences: the diſappointed king, at a more favourable ſeaſon, obtained an Act of Parliament, which reflects equal honour on the promoter and the Chriſtian cauſe. In 1689 the Act of Toleration came forth, intituled, " An Act " for exempting their Majeſties Proteſtant Sub- " jects, diſſenting from the Church of England, " from the Penalties of certain Laws," &c*.

It is from this memorable period that the diſſenters date that liberty and indulgence which they now enjoy, and have ſo long been bleſſed with; and it might have been expected that an experience of the fatal effects of former religious conflicts, and the benefits of an enlarged and liberal toleration, would have ſealed the tranquillity of the kingdom. But, as it has been already obſerved, in proportion to the ſtability of the Engliſh government, religious faction has been often found to thrive: ſo, in the period immediately ſubſequent to the revolution, although no open hoſtilities were offered to the eſtabliſhment, nor any abſurd application made by the diſſenters for a repeal of thoſe

---

* In this bill the Corporation and Teſt Acts are omitted, and conſequently remain in force.

laws

laws which they, by their own voluntary acquiescence had so recently sanctioned *; yet, so favourable was this period to fanatical conceit, that we find a multitude of sects starting up afresh, and again involving the people in the perplexities of controversy and division.

The clemency which was now extended to the dissenters in England, was not enjoyed by their brethren in the neighbouring kingdoms. In Ireland an intolerant spirit raged amongst the sectaries, and they suffered persecution, not as schismatics from the established church, but as dissenters from their own narrow creeds and formularies. The fate of Mr. Thomas Emlyn, a learned but unhappy Unitarian, sufficiently illustrates this matter. His dissenting brethren having discovered some heterodox opinion of his, respecting the incomprehensible mystery of the Trinity, applied, with unexampled assurance, to that government under which they themselves enjoyed *no legal toleration*, and actually obtained, in 1703, from sir Richard Pine, the then lord chief justice of Ireland, a special warrant to seize the miserable heretic and his papers; and, lest he should escape the just vengeance of the offended laws, the pious zealots conducted him in person to the common gaol of Newgate; there indeed they

---

* The political maxim of the celebrated Junius is not inapplicable to the present case: " The submission of a free people " to the executive authority of government, is no more than a " compliance with laws which they themselves have enacted." Letter 1.

left him: " for," as he says in the Narrative of his Life, " during my confinement all my acquaint-
" ance were estranged from me, and all offices of
" friendship and civility ceased; but of all men,
" the dissenting ministers of Dublin were the most
" destitute of kindness. Not one of them, except-
" ing Mr. Boyse, vouchsafed me so much as that
" small office of humanity, in visiting me when in
" prison: nor had they so much pity on the soul of
" their erring brother, as they thought him, as to
" seek to turn him from the error of his ways *."

In the same year, the kirk of Scotland had an opportunity of manifesting her zeal for *pure and undefiled religion*. Upon a motion of the earl of Strathmore's, the 6th of May 1703, " for the " toleration of all Protestants in the exercise of " religious worship," the presbyterians raised a violent and successful opposition; and, forgetful of the indulgence that their brethren at that time were enjoying under episcopacy in England, rejected the motion with horror, exclaiming against such *sinful communion*, and declaring that to enact a toleration in favour of episcopalians, would be to *establish iniquity by law*.

It would be foreign to my design to enter into a detail of the religious controversies, or the intestine broils, that harrassed the kingdom during the reign

* See Narrative of his Life prefixed to his Works, and Biograph. Dict. article Emlyn.—This gentleman afterwards fled for shelter to England, and became an intimate friend of the famous Dr. Samuel Clarke.

of queen Anne. The violent conduct of two turbulent parties disgraced this period of English history; for religion, from the first rise of the Whig and Tory factions, was always brought in as a pretext to cover the political views of either party*. The dissenters, who now constituted a great part of the Whig faction, under an idle pretence that the court and Tory party were solicitous to restore the Pretender, uniformly opposed the measures of the latter, and provoked them, after two unsuccessful attempts, to bring in and pass a bill † *to prevent occasional conformity*, and also ‡ *an act to prevent the growth of schism*, in order more effectually to humble those *dangerous schismatics*, as they affected to call their Whig opponents. These bills, however, were in reality a species of persecution, and a heavy clog on that free toleration granted at the revolution; but they originated in the turbulence of party, and

---

* The church was not a little distracted by the indecent contests amongst the clergy, who ranged themselves under two divisions, distinguished by the titles of High Church and Low Church. These ecclesiastical Whigs and Tories loaded each other with the most invidious epithets; the high-church men stigmatized their opponents as republicans and presbyterians, whilst their low-church brethren branded their adversaries with the appellation of Jacobites, and enemies to the revolution. And these odious contests, being fomented not a little by the Dissenters, contributed in the end to fetter toleration with illiberal restrictions. They served also to furnish a very celebrated orator, near fourscore years afterwards, with argument to wound the credit of the present hierarchy; but he was *more happy in his recollection* of these odious disputes, than he was *certain te in his application* of them to the subject under debate: March 3d, 1790.

† In 1711. ‡ In 1714.

would

would not have stained the clemency of this reign, if the dissenters had not been so forward in promoting political feuds*. We are now arrived at a period of our history favourable to genius and literary merit. The progress of reason, and a liberal cultivation of the mental powers, had not only freed the human mind from the shackles of Romish superstition, but rendered a relapse into popery morally impossible. From the influence of that unbounded liberty which each individual now claimed of speaking and writing on theological subjects, it was natural to expect an increase of sectaries; and accordingly we find the most absurd and ridiculous opinions broached among the people, whilst enthusiasm, under the affectation of superior sanctity, hung upon the skirts of pure religion.

From the whimsical attacks of imposture and fanaticism the church felt little annoyance; but a false philosophy, which had leagued itself with the-

---

* That there were several schemes, at the latter part of this reign, to restore the pretender to the crown, cannot be doubted; but that the queen, or the Tory party, were the instruments of such a design, does not at all appear by their conduct. It is certain that the queen had some Jacobites about her, who secretly wished for such a revolution: but that the Tories could be brought to engage in, or even to favour, so absurd a measure, there is not the least foundation to suppose. Party writers have copied this inconsistent charge one after another, and designedly overlooked the spirited intention of the Tories to rescue their sovereign from a certain domestic slavery which held her. They should have reflected that the Jacobite party would not have been so hardy as to counsel these men to alter that succession which they had so lately established.

ology,

ology, began now to wound the credit of revelation, and the interests of the orthodox faith. The malignant hypotheses of Hutcheson and Collins, of Tindal and of Chubb, were received in this æra of free-thinking with wonderful applause; their disciples were numerous, and the intoxicating fumes of free enquiry shook the conviction of the unstable, slackened the activity of the orthodox, and seduced many from the simplicity of the gospel.

The established church indeed had few or no open enemies to contend with, in the beginning of this century; nevertheless, under pretence of freedom of enquiry, and the exercise of reason, its tranquillity was wounded, and the crude fancies of infidels and fanatics obtruded on its members. For with the liberty of religious worship, the licentiousness of enthusiasm and infidelity encreased; and such was the insolence and effrontery of the sceptics of these days, that the good sense of the nation was offended by their bold attacks on the being of a God, the credibility of the gospel, and the dignity of the Christian cause; whilst the most respectable members of the church were insulted by the profane wit and blasphemous ridicule of deists and of atheists *.—Thus, although we impute the progress

---

* Such was the freedom of thinking and writing on religious points at this time, that the effusions of impiety and extravagance, which were poured forth among the people, were more greedily sought after and read than the manly productions of an enlightened clergy. And it is a fact, that the profane writings of

gress of the protestant faith to the improvements in science and philosophy, yet we cannot forget, that with the cultivation of the human powers the subtilties of dialectics, and the mischievous refinements of metaphysical argument were introduced. No period had been so favourable as the present to literary merit; and genius, although not much encouraged by the great, flourished under the culture of a liberal public; for, as a philosophical spirit of free enquiry had diffused itself amongst the people, metaphysical reasonings, however precarious and unsatisfactory, obtained an inauspicious homage: and it was, no doubt, in reference to this speculative knowledge, that an acute defender of the Dissenters was led to think, " That improvements in " philosophy have made many sceptics in all " churches, reformed and unreformed *."

The ascendency which this spirit of free enquiry had gained over the minds of men, and the reputation which philosophy had now attained by the discoveries of exalted genius and superior talents, contributed in no small degree to the culture of sophistry and scepticism. True philosophy, indeed, like pure religion, will rise the brighter from the researches and

of Toland, Mandeville, Woolston, &c. were so coveted, that some of these needy sceptics gleaned a comfortable subsistence from the corruptions of the age, and their booksellers, notwithstanding some expensive law-suits, which these productions had involved them in, acquired considerable sums by the sale of their multiplied absurdities.

* Preface to the Confessional, p. 60.

enquiries of real genius; but, under the name of science, falsely so called, a profusion of wild chimæras and specious systems were now obtruded on the public, and their reception was favourable, because they were adorned with all the elegance of fancy. The powers and genius of those real philosophers, Bacon, Newton, and Boyle, were not only exerted in the investigations of experimental and natural knowledge, but were directed to the evidences and confirmation of the great truths of Christianity[*]; whilst some overweening sophists, assuming the dignity of philosophy and a resemblance of these real sages, pointed their feeble science at the credit of revelation. The subtilties of metaphysics were at this time mistaken for the depth of real wisdom, and because men wanted discernment, they yielded

---

[*] The friends of Arianism and Socinianism have alternately claimed this great man as their own. Whiston represented him as an Arian, and has candour enough to tell us, in the Memoirs of his own life, that Sir Isaac Newton was so much offended with him for this, that he would never suffer him to enter as a member of the Royal Society, while he sat at the head of it. Dr. Priestley, in his turn, claims him as a Socinian. The fact is, this good man justly abhorred the persecution of the Non-conformists; and this was not inconsistent with his being firmly attached to the Church of England. He judged of *men by their manners*; and the true schismatics were, in his opinion, the vicious and the wicked; not that he confined his principles to natural religion, for he was thoroughly persuaded of the truths of revelation; and, amidst the great variety of books which he had constantly before him, that which he studied with the greatest application was the Bible. See Biog. Dict. article Newton; and Importance of Free Enquiry, &c. 109.

themselves easy vassals to imaginative science. The philosophical improvements of those great men threw a splendour over true religion, and the evangelical truths were illustrated and confirmed by their literary exertions: but the subtil refinements of Bolingbroke*, and *the civil, social, and theistic system*, which Shaftesbury † had derived from the antient moralists, were set up in opposition to the gospel of Christ; and the fine wit and elegant humour with which these visionaries had decked out their scepticism, was so well seasoned to the artificial taste and flimsy principles of the times, as to charm their numerous and deluded followers. Deism having thus assumed the title of philosophy, infidelity triumphed at the expence of reason and demonstration.

I have been induced to take this short view of the state of science and philosophy at the beginning of this century, in order to bring forward a description

---

* The Essays on Philosophy and Religion, which Lord Bolingbroke addressed to Pope, contained so many offensive things against revelation, that they occasioned a presentment of his works by the Grand Jury of Westminster.

† The Letters and Characteristics of Lord Shaftesbury are full of his visionary scheme of idolizing moral virtue, at the expence of revelation. Every page shews him a zealous asserter of the *civil, social, and theistic system*; and his philosophy was made up of two principles, viz. That there is a Providence which administers and consults for the whole, to the absolute exclusion of general evil and disorder; and, That man is made by that Providence a political or social animal, whose constitution can only find its true and natural end in the pursuit and exercise of the moral and social virtues. See Biog. Dict. article Cooper.

of Dissenters, whose political conduct has not been hitherto under consideration; my remarks having been in general confined to those non-conformists, the Presbyterians, Independents, Anabaptists, and Quakers, who, since the reformation, have made so conspicuous a figure in the popular commotions of this country. The *Unitarian system* having been little known in England until the middle of the last century, could not be considered as an object of political investigation; for, as these religionists made no figure in the community, but were dispersed amongst that great variety of sects that sprung up after the reformation, their theological tenets, or social conduct, had not excited much attention.—It is not my design, neither would it be consistent with my plan, to examine the doctrines of Unitarianism, or to discuss the merits of that faith, which would annihilate the dearest interests of Christianity*. I leave it to abler pens, and firmer nerves, to embark on this antipacific ocean of theological controversy; my business is with the Unitarian, as a subject and fellow-citizen, *although not of the*

---

* " Socinianism cuts to the very root of all that is distinguish-
" ing in the gospel. It destroys the necessity, and even the im-
" portance of a miraculous interposition, and gives the infidel
" too great reason to exclaim, that all that was extraordinary
" was superfluous; and that the apparatus was too expensive and
" too splendid for the purposes to which it was applied. This
" seems to be an argument à priori against that species of Christianity, which some, under the pretence of refining it from
" corruption, would reduce to the level of natural religion."
White's Sermons at the Bampton Lecture, notes, p. 68.

household

houſehold of faith; and I ſhall conſider his conduct, whether Arian or Socinian, as a member of that ſociety, which affords a liberal connivance at, but no legal toleration of, his creed *.

To the ſpirit of faction, and an ardent zeal for proſelytiſm, two evils equally offenſive to civil government, we are indebted for the riſe and progreſs of this ſpiritual contagion. Driven from a country, which had afforded them countenance and protection, by an offence againſt the civil and eccleſiaſtical eſtabliſhments † of it, the diſciples of Socinus directed their emiſſaries to ſearch out a reſting-place. England, that land of religious liberty, that hot-bed of ſectaries, was open to the wretched exiles, and here they found a refuge from thoſe continental ſtorms which their zeal and irregularities had

---

* The Socinians are not included in the Act of Toleration; and by the 9th and 10th of William III. they are expoſed to ſundry diſabilities. Likewiſe by the 13th Eliz. c. 12. and the 29th Ch. II. c. 9.

† Amongſt other acts of violence which their zeal has tempted them to commit, was that famous tumult at Racow, in Poland. Their rage for reformation was vented againſt an unfortunate crucifix, which had excited their religious reſentment, and which they ſo belaboured with ſticks and ſtones, that they at laſt triumphed in its overthrow. The matter, however, did not end here, the *reformers* attracted the notice of the civil magiſtrate, and they were baniſhed Poland with the utmoſt ignominy in 1638, for this breach of the peace; but they have always gloried in their zeal and their ſufferings. " As Chriſtians, we think it our duty to " hazard *every thing*, rather than neglect to take *any meaſures in* " *our power* to propagate truth." See Dr. Prieſtley's Letter to Mr. Pitt, p. 24.—1787.

gathered

gathered round them*. The emissaries then of this community are first discovered in this country towards the middle of the seventeenth century, in the course of which they gained many proselytes, some of whom were men of eminence and distinction: nor is

---

* The Unitarian religion, before the improvements of Faustus Socinus, was an incoherent ill-digested system; but the consummate abilities of this enterprising man disguised, in great measure, its former monstrous absurdities, and gave it an air of method and connexion. Hence, according to Dr. Mosheim, the modern Unitarians are very properly called Socinians. The term Unitarian, indeed, is very comprehensive, and is not only applied to the Arians and Socinians, but to all those who reject the doctrine of the Trinity, upon which the Church of England is established. Notwithstanding the address and dexterity of this able reformer, he could not preserve his community from intestine divisions. One more zealous than prudent, by his ardour and obstinacy in opposing the divine worship of Christ, brought upon himself the vengeance of the civil authority; and it was in vain that Socinus attempted to soften down the error of Francis Davides, whose offensive tenets were the occasion of his being thrown into prison, where he perished in 1579. Several others were banished the society, and suffered bitterly in the countries to which they had fled; but amongst them all, the capital errors of Budnæus gave most uneasiness to Socinus; and it called forth all his abilities to colour over the daring heresy of this man, who positively asserted, " That Christ was not begotten by any extraordinary act " of divine power, but that he was born like other men, and " tempted like other men." Hence he easily drew this deduction, " That to pay religious worship of any kind to Jesus " Christ was idolatry." This hypothesis, however conformable to the fundamental principles of Socinianism, was at this time looked upon as impious and intolerable; and he was induced afterwards to abandon these offensive sentiments, and was

again

is this to be wondered at, "For it is remarkable,
"that the Socinians, in propagating their religious
"principles, have always followed a quite different
"method from that which has been obſerved by
"other ſects. It has been the general practice of
"ſectaries and innovators to endeavour to render
"themſelves popular, and to begin by gaining the
"multitude to their ſide; but the diſciples of So-
"cinus, who are perpetually exalting the *dignity,*
"*prerogatives, and authority of reaſon,* have this
"peculiarity in their manner of proceeding, that
"they are at very little pains to court the favour

again re-admitted into the community from which he had been excommunicated. How far theſe opinions are held by modern Socinians may be beſt gathered from the tenets of their intrepid champion: "If, Sir, you ſuppoſe that all the clergy of the "Church of England really believe that Jeſus Chriſt is a proper "object of prayer, and that he is to be adjured by *his holy* "*Nativity, &c.* with many other doctrines *equally abhorrent to* "*reaſon,* you are greatly miſtaken." See letter to the Right Hon. William Pitt, p. 31.—"I am endeavouring by all the "means in my power, to rouſe the attention of thinking "men in this country to the corrupt ſtate of religion that is eſta- "bliſhed in it; and eſpecially to convince them of this miſ- "chievous tendency of *worſhipping Chriſt* as God." Letters to Dr. Horſley, part 3d.—This ſeems to be the Budnæan doctrine in perfection, and is enough to raiſe the ſpirit of the *gentler* Socinus. Whether an expoſtulation would prevail with his diſciple to change his principles, or to abandon thoſe tenets, which are neither to be found in the Creed of Fauſtus, nor the Catechiſm of Cracow, may beſt be collected from the words of his zealous votary: "This is more than I would chuſe to ſay of my own "opinions. I may ſee reaſon to change them to-morrow." Importance of Free Enquiry, notes, p. 109.—1785.

"of

"of the people, or to make proselytes to their
"cause among those who are not distinguished
"from the multitude by their rank or their abili-
"ties. It is only among the learned and the great
"that they seek for disciples and patrons with a
"zealous assiduity *."

Agreeable to these principles, they instructed their disciples, in their famous academy at Racow, in the rules of eloquence and rhetoric, and paid great attention to the subtilties of philosophy and logic; by which means they invited the notice of men of birth and distinction, who, in this dawn of science, were fond of patronizing persons of education and talents, and who insensibly became members of their community. The like causes produced the like effects in this our country. When speculative philosophy had spread its influence amongst us, and when we had set up the *lamp of reason*, as the only infallible guide to truth, the Unitarian principles could not fail of a favourable reception.—The season I have pointed out; the success let us next attend to.

Christianity had, at the period under contemplation, many enemies to contend with; the nation had been overrun with scepticism and infidelity, and every sense of religion seemed to be extinguished in the minds of men. Atheism, indeed, began to droop, for the daring impieties of Hobbes and Spinoza had excited general disgust, and the public willingly received a refutation of the absurd *denial*

* Mosheim's Ecclef. Hist. by Maclane, vol. v. p. 52.

of the existence and moral government of an all-powerful Being, even from the hands of Deism itself; which *scrupled only at the divine origin of the gospel,* but promoted a religion which was to *be amenable to the dictates of natural reason.* Here was ample room for the Unitarian missionary; his fundamental maxim, " That all things that surpass the limits " of human comprehension, should be entirely ba- " nished from the Christian religion," could not fail of accommodating this *philosophic age.* The harvest truly was plenteous, the reapers were at hand, and the sickle was thrust in with no little success*. To stop the progress of infidelity, the legislature interfered, and the 9th† and 10th statutes of William III. came forth to prevent the total subversion of religion and morality.

Having

---

* The reader who would wish to see an account of the Unitarian church, may consult a candid and liberal publication of Mr. Lindsey, entitled, " An Historical View of the State of the " Unitarian Doctrine and Worship, from the Reformation to our " own Times." 1783.

† It is worthy notice, that this statute seems to be pointed at those who have apostatized from Christianity : " If any person, " having been educated in, or at any time having made profession " of the Christian religion within this realm, shall, by writing, " printing, &c. deny any one of the persons in the Holy Tri- " nity to be God, &c. or shall deny the Christian religion to be " true, or the scriptures to be of divine authority, &c." And it seems to have a peculiar respect to those who, having embraced Socinianism, by a very natural transition passed into Deism, and ended in downright Atheism. Such was the case of the unsettled Toland ; his first step was Socinianism, which appeared in his

book,

Having thus brought forward the Unitarian to public notice, I shall leave him for a while, blended in the common mass of Protestant Dissenters, and resume my subject. Perhaps I may have incurred some censure for this digression, and been thought to have wandered from my original undertaking, which was, "to contrast the late friend-
"ly professions of the Dissenters with their former
"political conduct." This censure might be applicable to a less desultory publication; in the present case I claim indulgence under the sanction of a celebrated critic. "Memoirs denote a compo-
"sition, in which an author does not pretend to
"give full information of all the facts respecting
"the period of which he writes, but only to relate
"what he himself had access to know, or what he
"was concerned in, or what illustrates the conduct

---

book, entitled, "Christianity not mysterious," and from hence he proceeded gradually, through the medium theism, to the summit of infidelity.

It is this famous statute that is the bugbear of Dr. Priestley: " Repeal the act of king William, which makes it blasphemy " to impugn the doctrine of the Trinity. I think *it my duty* to " attempt the utter overthrow of this doctrine." Letter to Pitt, p. 24.—But let him calm his fears, if *he really has any*, and let him rest quiet, as a social being, as a citizen, and subject; and, I dare pledge myself, that he will not be dignified by persecution or martyrdom. Church of England men are of the same metal with the Athenians of old, who condemned Socrates, not for saying, " *There is but one God,*" but for his imprudently exciting a sedition in order to overthrow the established worship of his country. See Voltaire's Letters concerning the English Nation.

" of

" of some person, or the circumstances of some
" transaction, which he chuses for his subject.
" From a writer of Memoirs, therefore, is not ex-
" pected the same profound research, or enlarged
" information, as from a writer of History. He is
" not subject to the same laws of unvarying dig-
" nity and gravity. He may talk freely of him-
" self: he may descend into the most familiar anec-
" dotes *."

By the several acts of parliament which had previously established the Protestant succession in the
house of Hanover, George I. found an easy and
peaceable accession to the throne †. The Protestant Dissenters having felt the benefits of Toleration,
and sensible of the blessings of a mild administration, dreaded, in common with their fellow-subjects, an interference of papal policy, and re-intro-

---

* Blair's Lectures on Rhetoric, &c. vol. iii. p. 52.

† In 1714.—The Dissenters are fond of charging the clergy of the Establishment with disaffection to the Protestant succession in the house of Brunswick. When the convention of estates, at the revolution, declared the throne to be vacant, and that the next Protestant heirs of the blood royal of Charles I. should fill the vacant throne, in the old order of succession, it has never been denied that many of the clergy, together with a great number of the people, from a regard to the antient line, looked with coolness on the temporary exception, or preference to the person of king William the third; and this unlucky prejudice was kept alive in the succeeding reigns by the contending interests of two powerful factions, to the great reputation, it seems, of the Dissenters of the present times!

duction

duction of arbitrary government. Accordingly, at a critical juncture *, when the tranquillity of the kingdom was interrupted by the hostile attempts of the pretender, their gratitude united with their self-interest in opposing the common enemy; and their allegiance was not long after rewarded by the removal of those restrictions which their political interference had brought upon them in the preceding reign †.

The reins of government devolved on George II. at a period equally propitious to the monarch and the subject ‡. The odious jealousies which had subsisted in the former reigns began to subside, and commerce, the idol of the nation, flowed naturally

---

* In the rebellion in 1715.

† The Occasional conformity and Schism Acts were repealed in 1718.

‡ In 1727.—When the death of George the first was made known, a council was assembled at Leicester-house, where his majesty made a declaration, in which was the following expression: " *The religion, laws, and liberties* of the kingdom are most dear " to me: and the *preservation* of the constitution in church and " state, as *it is now happily established,* shall be my first and al- " ways my chief care."

It has been often asserted by the advocates of the Dissenters, that the princes of the house of Hanover have been always zealous for the repeal of the Tests. The sagacious author of the Confessional roundly affirms, that the " attempts which were " made in the reigns of George I. and George II. *to repeal the* " *Tests,* did not miscarry for want of the *hearty concurrence of the* " *princes on the throne."* Pref. to the Confessional, p. 50.—And the ingenious Asserter of the Rights of the Protestant Dissenters insinuates

turally through all her channels. Civil liberty, and the rights of mankind, were now clearly understood, and national prosperity promised a lasting duration. The declaration to maintain the constitution as established by law, which the king made at the commencement of his reign, prepossessed his subjects in his favour, and was a pledge of his future intentions to protect the establishment, and to secure the subject in the exercise of his civil and religious freedom. The political ferments that afterwards disturbed this reign were not a little increased by the irregular conduct and unexpected claims of the Protestant Dissenters.

We have seen them grateful for the blessings of a free Toleration, and, mindful only of their spiritual concerns, making no attempts to overleap those barriers, or to demolish those fences, which the wisdom and policy of their forefathers had peaceably acquiesced in. Some malcontents, in a populous commercial town, first discovered the imperfection of the state machine, and, zealous, no doubt,

---

insinuates, that the *private* sentiments of Sir Robert Walpole, though he opposed the motion for the repeal, which was brought into the house by Mr. Walter Plummer, in 1736, were favourable to the application. The direct contrary of this is the fact: Sir Robert Walpole, together with that most independent of men, Mr. Shippen, opposed the motion strenuously, upon these very grounds: "That a repeal of those clauses in the Test Act, which "require those who are admitted into offices to take the Sacra- "ment, would be *extremely dangerous to the established church*. See Rights of the Prot. Diss. asserted, p. 29.

for

for the *salus reipublicæ*, and *the rights of their fellow-citizens*, undertook to infuse new health and new vigour into the diseased constitution *; or,

> "Blushing that the world went well, had rather,
> "Though they themselves did suffer by it, beheld
> "Dissentious numbers pest'ring streets, than see
> "Their tradesmen singing in their shops, and going
> "About their functions friendly."   CORIOLANUS.

The object of these state physicians was to remove the sacramental tests; and they drew this

---

* "In 1731 the Dissenters of Liverpool determined to apply to the legislature for relief. That they might have the greater chance of success, they proposed a general application of the Dissenters when the *parliament should be drawing to a close*; and hoped that, to secure their influence at the approaching general election, the minister might be induced to hazard something in their favour.—In many counties and towns they entered into engagements mutually to support, as candidates, *the friends of civil and religious liberty, and the house of Hanover.*" See Rights of Prot. Diff. asserted, p. 28.

About this time the Dissenters in Ireland attempted to obtain a repeal of the Test Act. These men often affected to call themselves brother Protestants and fellow Christians with the members of the established church. Upon this occasion Dean Swift wrote a short copy of verses, which so provoked one Bettesworth, a lawyer, and member of the Irish establishment, that he swore, in the hearing of many persons, to revenge himself either by murdering or maiming the Dean. And for this purpose he engaged some ruffians to assault him, wherever they could find him. This lawless attempt roused the nobility and gentry of the liberty of St. Patrick's, who, in a body, waited on the Dean, and presented a paper subscribed with their names, in which they solemnly engaged to defend his person and fortune, as the friend and benefactor of his country, against the insults of this furious Dissenter. See Biog. Dict. article Swift.

patriotic

patriotic inference, which their descendants probably will never forget, that when the obnoxious clauses in the Test Act were done away, their distressed country, would be no longer deprived of their political abilities. To aid the scheme of reformation, the Quaker caught the spirit of faction, and joining the patriots, preferred, about the same time, his *humble petition* for a relief from the *payment of tythes, church rates, and all other ecclesiastical dues* *.

The ferment which these unconstitutional claims † had occasioned greatly disconcerted the reigning prince,

---

* The Dissenters did not find *a fit time* to bring forward their motion for a repeal of the Test Act till 1736, when it was lost by a majority of 251 against 123. Another effort was made in 1739, but this was quashed by a still greater proportionate majority, viz. 188 to 89. The Quakers met with better success; the bill that was brought in for their relief, after much altercation passed the Commons, but was thrown out by the Lords; however,

" Both parties join'd to do their best,
" To damn the public interest;
" To try at both ends of the saw,
" And tear down government and law."
Hudib. Cant. 3.

The established church was at this time greatly indebted to the services of Dr. Gibson, bishop of London, who, by timely apprizing the clergy of the bold scheme of the Quakers, to deprive them of their legal maintenance by tithes, and by animating his brethren on the bench to concur with him, averted a serious blow, that was aimed at religion, and the rights and properties of the clergy.

† I maintain that their claims are *unconstitutional*, however the term may be combated by sophistry. If the ancestors of the Dissenters

prince, who, about this time, intending to visit his German dominions, and dreading the consequences of such internal contests, closed the session of 1736 with this paternal admonition. "He expressed great concern at seeing such seeds of dissension sown among his people: He declared it was his desire, and should ever be his care, to preserve the present constitution in church and state as by law established: and recommended a spirit of harmony and concord among all the Protestants of the nation, as the *chief support of the happy Establishment.*"

I forbear commenting on this authentic document, and shall only remark that it completely refutes those assertions of the Protestant Dissenters, "That their principles have been uniformly friendly to the Establishment." Had they been so even at this period, they would not have received this sort of counsel from a prince, the avowed friend to religious toleration. A compleat defeat which the cause of the Protestant Dissenters sustained in a second effort to obtain their unconstitutional demands, in 1739, silenced their clamours, and we hear little or nothing of imaginary grievances for the remainder of this reign.

Dissenters did assist in the contrivance and settlement of that scheme of government, generally understood by the British Constitution, and helped to establish *or confirm* certain Tests, as necessary to the preservation of it, (a circumstance easily proved) every attempt to overthow those essential principles, on which such settlement is founded, may fairly be deemed unconstitutional.

Having

Having brought those transactions of the Protestant Dissenters, which relate to their supposed attachment to the Establishment of this country, down to our own times, I shall make a momentary pause, in order to apprise my reader, that I have not selected these historical remarks, with a view to cloud his judgment, or to inflame his resentments against the Dissenters as such. I am as averse as any man, from drawing unfavourable conclusions of the principles of a party, from the opinions, or *even the actions of a few* of that party, much less from the suspicions of their adversaries. But when I see their *Resolutions*, their Pamphlets, and popular declamations swelled out with ostentatious references to former loyalty and attachment; when I am told by their celebrated orator*, " That the law considers no man's opinion to be " injurious, until such opinion be brought *into* " *action*;" and am instructed by their literary champion †, " to judge of principles, as our Sa- " viour teaches us to judge of men, *by their ac-* " *tions*," however unwilling I may be to recur to periods, when a narrow and contracted policy governed the actions of mankind, yet, when I see the whole collected body of the Dissenters pressing forward for the removal of the antient Tests of the constitution, under the colourable pretext of political merit, it becomes, in justice to their own posi-

---

* See Mr. Fox's speech in the house of Commons, March 3, 1790.

† Importance of Free Enquiry, p. 106.

tion, and in compliance with their own doctrine, a necessary although an invidious task, to appeal to the page of history for an estimate of Dissenting-principles. In the prosecution of this enquiry, it will appear to the impartial reader, that my facts are, for the most part, collected from authors the declared friends to toleration; and the result of the argument is, that the merit so arrogantly assumed, is to be resolved into a self-interested principle, a self-interest in maintaining a government, which extends to all its subjects equal security and protection.

Civil government is an institution in which we are all confederated for mutual safety and defence, and the interests of the community indispensably require the *active* exertions of *every individual*, however differing in religious sentiments, when the general safety is at stake. But, as the religious interests of the Protestant Dissenters are interwoven with the establishment of the Church of England, their indifference at the time when the latter was threatened with the hostilities of a foreign enemy, and with the revival of papal intolerance, would have hazarded their own cause; and their neutrality would have been a political crime of great magnitude.

Sensible and considerate men will see through this sophistry, and be tempted to conclude, that a self-interested attachment has been the chief foundation of Dissenting patriotism!

We are now entering upon a period of our history, dear to every lover of his country; a period that posterity will envy us the enjoyment of, and which the children that are yet unborn will contemplate with fond veneration and regard. Our beloved monarch George III. ascended the throne, amidst the acclamations of a prosperous and happy people: the early specimen * which he gave of his serious determination to promote religion and virtue, and to preserve and strengthen the constitution both in church and state †, promised an augmentation of social happiness, and the maintenance of political privileges; and an undeviating attention to these original professions has marked the progress of this illustrious reign. Acts of indemnity and indulgence to the Dissenters followed these favourable appearances, and we find them at this time truly sensible of a mild and beneficent administration ‡.

---

* See the proclamation for the encouragement of piety and virtue, issued in 1760.

† Address to the council assembled at Carlton-house. State Papers.

‡ The Dissenters, in expectation of the fullness of their wishes, affect to scout the very idea of an indemnity act. Strange perverseness! was it not for these remittances, their clamours would be louder, and with greater degree of reason. Neither do they attribute the indulgences and the tranquillity they enjoyed at this period to political influence, but to an unnatural sensation: " Our gracious monarch George III. ascended " the throne in 1760, and from that time *an unaccountable torpor* " *has seized the Dissenters.*" Right of Protestant Dissenters asserted, sect. 7.

The strange attempt that had been made in the preceding reign, to obtain a repeal of the Test-laws, though at that time alarming, contributed eventually to this general harmony. The arguments that were then adduced by Sherlock, Warburton, Gibson, and others, had so completely evinced the necessity of preserving certain Tests, as bulwarks of the constitution, that the opinions of men were well made up upon the subject; and the determined resolution of administration to defend the Establishment upon this principle, together with the decided majorities in the legislature against these unconstitutional demands, warranted an expectation that the subject would not be revived, as long at least as the memory of the transaction should remain. Accordingly we find half a century lapse in the tranquil enjoyment of religious privilege.

A dread of the fatal consequences of intestine feuds, and a just abhorrence of persecution for conscience sake, contributed, with the encreasing spirit of Toleration, to suppress former animosities and disaffection. The old narrowness of superstitious policy, had shrunk before the milder influence of lenity, and mutual forbearance: and churchmen now freely acknowledged, that the tenets of Christianity, and the doctrines of their own Establishment, contained the strongest arguments for toleration; that humanity and benevolence, so forcibly enjoined by each, could not consist with an arbitrary compulsion into established forms of worship;
and

and that the intercourse betwixt God, and a man's own conscience should be free and uncontrouled.

In times so favourable to religious liberty, it was natural for Dissenters to press forward for the fullness of indulgence, and the removal of all restrictions; and in the progress of this reign we find them petitioning for, and obtaining an extension of privilege, and an avowed completion of their wishes. In 1777 certain disabilities, under which the ministers of the Protestant Dissenters laboured, were removed, and so sensible were they of the favour and relief granted them in this instance, that a leading and truly respectable character * amongst them

---

* Dr. Kippis, see his letter.—In the debate on Mr. Fox's motion, March 3d, 1790, Mr. Pitt with great success pressed this argument on the house, contending, "that, as the Protestant Dissenters had, at the time this relief was granted to them, declared in the most public manner, that they had nothing more to ask of the legislature, and were now, in direct contradiction, urging additional demands on Parliament—it was impossible to judge how far they meant to proceed, or what would in fact content them." Yet this fair reasoning was parried with singular address by Mr. Beaufoy: he allowed that at the time alluded to, the Dissenters were satisfied, and expressed themselves so; but then, as those indulgences affected them *as ministers*, they were not precluded coming forward in the present instance *as men!* Such equivocation is neither candid, nor indeed politic. And as the Dissenters have already urged the justice of their being exonerated of ecclesiastical fees, in order to transfer them to their own ministry, it is reasonable to expect, from this instance of mental reservation, that they will in time come forward for a legal establishment to secure to their clergy this voluntary tribute.

declared, " That they had now no additional claims to urge, and that their toleration was complete *.

The approved clemency of the monarch, and the mildness of an enlightened age, encouraged another description of Dissenters, equally well affected to the civil constitution of this country, to solicit a remission of their grievances, and an abatement of real persecution; and such was the success of the modest and reasonable petition of the Roman Catholics, that in 1778 they obtained, without opposition, a repeal of the 11th and 12th of William III. which, however necessary at the time of enacting, were now understood to be a disgrace to the statute book, and an offence to the feelings of a polished nation †.

These

---

* The redress so readily granted to the ministers of the Protestant Dissenters was but ill requited by one of their reverend body. A celebrated Unitarian, of revolution principles, added not a little to the calamities that distracted the kingdom about this time; his numerous inflammatory publications fomented the American revolt, and contributed in no small degree to the dismemberment of the empire. Whatever unforeseen advantages the nation may have received from this revolution, and they are not a few, the house of Brunswick will hardly thank this political Dissenter for his loyalty and allegiance.

† The penalties which were now repealed went to the punishment of Popish bishops and priests for officiating in the service of their church: the imprisoning Papists who kept schools, or educated and boarded youth: and the disabling Papists to inherit lands.

The Roman Catholics are still under great disabilities and penalties, by many acts passed from the 23d Eliz. to 11th of

George

These relaxations and abatements, originating in justice, and founded in policy, produced an occurrence as unexpected as it was atrocious. The outrages committed in 1780, by bands of desperate and designing men, under pretence of defending

---

George II. They are prohibited from teaching schools unless licensed by the ordinary. They cannot present to any advowson. If they say mass the fine is 200 marks, if they hear it 100 marks, and each suffers one year's imprisonment. They can hold no office nor employment. They must not keep arms, nor come within ten miles of London, on pain of 100 pounds. They can bring no action at law, nor suit in equity. If they travel five miles from home they forfeit all their goods. If they come to court they forfeit 100 pounds. If they send any person abroad to be educated in the Popish religion, or contribute towards it, the sender, the sent, and the contributor are disabled to sue in law or equity, to take any legacy, to bear any office, and forfeit all their goods and chattels, and all their real estate for life. If a Protestant becomes a convert to popery, or procures others to be so, the offence is high treason. These are real penalties and disabilities! penalties worth petitioning a remission of! and not a tittle of these affect the Protestant Dissenters. And yet how different is the conduct of the parties as citizens and subjects! From the Protestant Dissenters we hear nothing else but clamour and dissatisfaction, complaints of oppression and persecution, of fancied pains and imaginary grievances. Whilst the Roman Catholic appears contented under this heavy catalogue of penalties. Nay he is grateful for the clemency shewn him by an enlightened people, and even applauds that establishment which the Protestant Dissenter so incessantly reprobates. "Let us then remain as we are; for a better establishment, as I have said, more consonant with the rights of the people, and the prerogative of the crown, England can never enjoy." Such are the sentiments of a very eminent Catholic, in pleading the cause and interests of Dissenters! See Berrington on the Rights of the Dissenters.

the Protestant religion from the encroachments of Popery, excited the horror and indignation of mankind. I would not revive the memory of these excesses, if they had not a very close relation to the subject under discussion.

I am aware that the Protestant Dissenters will deny their being the authors of this horrible insurrection; and that their *principles*, in the present times, could not lead them to commit such atrocious *actions:* the latter part of this position rests with me to prove; what their *principles* were at this time may be fairly collected from a statement of them by a candid and impartial *Dissenting Minister*. " The diligent and impartial inquirer,
" however candid, must acknowledge that the
" Protestant Dissenters, in less time than even half
" a century past, were in general austere in their
" temper and manners; that they painted religion
" with a gloomy aspect; betrayed a spirit of sin-
" gularity and opposition in trifles; were excef-
" sive, and almost indiscriminate, in their invec-
" tives against pleasure; laid too much stress
" upon modes and opinions; made too little al-
" lowance for human infirmities; fixed too high a
" value on long and frequent retirements for the
" sake of devotional exercises in private; placed
" as much too low the standard of the *moral vir-*
" *tues*, those especially which are *humane, generous*,
" and of all others the most engaging: confined
" almost all their approbation and good-will to
" *the people of their own sect*; discovered an over-
" weening

"weening conceit of their own spiritual attain-
"ments; and—what is still worse than all the rest!
"—that there were undoubtedly instances of those
"who put on the semblance of rigorous piety to
"atone for, conceal, and give success to heinous
"immorality.—It is with all readiness acknow-
"ledged, that there are upon record many ex-
"ceptions to this heavy charge; but the above-
"mentioned may, I think, be exhibited as some
"of the principal outlines in the character of those
"who were, or affected to be, amongst the best
"and religious persons of the last age. Nay,
"further, if a diligent and impartial inquiry *were
"now made* (viz. 1780) into *the prevailing temper
"of large bodies of Protestant Dissenters*, in several
"different parts of this kingdom, it would be
"found, that something of *the same spirit is still
"amongst us* *."—Such are the *principles* of Protestant Dissenters, delineated in a fair, impartial
manner, by their own hands!

But I am far from imputing the fatal consequences of this terrible outrage solely to the Dissenters. I am sensible too, that many eminent
characters amongst them were consulted upon the
repeal of the 11th and 12th of William, and were
zealous in the cause of religious freedom, promoting the indulgence which the Catholics at this
time received. But, whilst justice is due to this
description of men for their candour and mode-

---

* See a Discourse on religious Zeal, by Mr. Rd. Godwin,
1780—bound up with two other Discourses.

ration,

ration, I cannot suppress my abhorrence of that tumultuous association of Protestant Dissenters, which, under the specious mask of patriotism and religion, first promoted an insurrection that subverted the civil authority, and introduced a scene of riot and disorder, that filled the empire with amazement and consternation.

Whatever * the real design of these infatuated men might be, the measures which they adopted to promote their cause were, in the leading features, so similar to the late attempt of the Protestant Dissenters to obtain a redress of their imaginary grievances, that I cannot in this place overlook the striking resemblance.

In

---

* Although the whole charge of these evils is not imputable to the Dissenters, yet the original and chief cause of the insurrection rests with them. It is a fact, that, so early as 1779, the infatuated leader of the rioters (lord George Gordon) maintained a correspondence with some disaffected teachers in Edinburgh and Dumfries, upon the subject of the Catholic Bill, and particularly with the president of a formidable body at Glasgow, called *The eighty-five Societies*, with whose agents this unhappy man was, in the following year, more closely connected, when he headed the Scotch division of insurgents in St. George's Fields, and proceeded with them in a tumultuous manner to Palace Yard, in order to intimidate the legislature into a compliance with their wishes, which then appeared to be a repeal of an act passed in 1778, disannulling the obnoxious clauses in the 11th and 12th of William, and admitting their fellow-subjects to some immunities. Besides the petition of the Protestant Associators, there were others, from various parts of the kingdom, presented by lord George Gordon, on behalf of the Dissenters, at the bar of the house of commons. An adherent

of

In 1780 the leaders of the infurrection, as a previous ftep, invited the notice of the public by circulating pamphlets, hand-bills, and public advertifements *, " exhorting the *true friends* of " Great Britain to unite, before it be too late, in " *vindication of civil and religious liberty.*"—In 1789 a fimilar ftep was taken by the Proteftant Diffenters, previous to the difcuffion of their caufe, and, at fome of their meetings, they ferioufly refolved " to raife a fund to defray the expences of " publifhing *fmall pieces in vindication of liberty* †."

Charity forbids my imputing to the firft affociators an intention of kindling a flame of fuch horror

---

of this gentleman's, and with whom he at that time lodged, was very roughly handled by Mr. Burke, in the debate on the petitions againft the Catholic Bill, 20th June, 1780. He attacked this gentleman (alderman Bull) with great feverity " for the " part *he had acted in the late difturbances,* and for his fupport" ing the petitions againft the Catholics." He afked, " How " fuch a man as he, enjoying as *a Proteftant Diffenter all the* " *bleffings of religious Toleration,* could reconcile it to his con" fcience to deny fome few comforts to other men, between " whom and him there was no difference but the mere diffe" rence of religious opinion ?"—From thefe and a multitude of other reafons we may fairly conclude, that the riots of 1780 were promoted and conducted by Proteftant Diffenters.

* See the various advertifements of the Proteftant Affociators, in the periodical papers of 1780.

† From amongft others of the fame import, I felect the following refolution of the meeting of Proteftant Diffenters at Bolton in Lancafhire, 17th of December, 1789: " That, as " nothing can be *more beneficial to a good caufe* than promoting " a knowledge of its merits, it be recommended to the Affembly
" of

ror and devastation from so small a spark; or to the second a *presentiment* of the consequences of their injudicious publications. In the first case, indeed, the invaders of the public peace witnessed the mischief which their inflammatory notices had excited, and attempted, when too late, to retrieve the unhappy step they had taken *: from the latter *prelude to sedition*, we have hitherto experienced no evil consequences.

If

---

* of Delegates for this district, to endeavour to raise a fund from
" among the congregations which they represent, to defray the
" expence of publishing *small pieces in vindication of liberty*, and
" the rights of the Dissenters."—And, in consequence of these resolutions, *small pieces*, of a *peculiar tendency*, were published in February 1790, and advertised *for circulation* at 5 s. per hundred.

* The Protestant Dissenters in 1780, finding that it was easier to assemble than to appease a mob by hand-bills, thought proper, when their partizans were proceeding to outrageous lengths, to publish counter-notices, dissuading the insurgents from their excesses; and, in fact, disavowing all connection with them if they proceeded further. And their unhappy leader attempted, at his examination before the privy council, to exculpate himself by saying, that " he could not *foresee* the mischief
" that had ensued." Yet here was some apparent contrition, some palliation of the offence; and however slight, the most favourable construction was put upon it. But the Protestant Dissenters of 1790, although admonished by some of their moderate and rational brethren not to proceed to such unjustifiable lengths as their resolutions held forth, in contempt of the friendly admonition, plainly intimated, that their first exertions, their *small pieces in vindication of liberty*, were only a prelude to nobler atchievements. This appeared clearly from a letter which Mr. Burke produced in the house of commons, March 3d, 1790, in

the

If I should be thought to have used, on this occasion, an expression too harsh, let it be remembered that allegiance to the state may be broken by other means than by open acts of rebellion: the circulating small publications, calculated to inspire the people with disaffection to the existing laws and government, however cautiously worded, may very fairly be deemed a *prelude to sedition*; for the guilt of popular insurrection consists as much in any act promotive of the tumult, as in the real injury done to the community: and this species of libel, as it inflames the passions, is generally productive of disorder. In the first instance, we have seen it lead a deluded mob to the destruction of the lives and properties of their fel-

---

the debate on Mr. Fox's motion: this letter he declared he had received but the day before, from a Mr. Fletcher, a Dissenter in Lancashire; in which he stated, "that the meeting of Pro-"testant Dissenters held at Bolton avowed such violent prin-"ciples, that he would not stay, but came away with some other "moderate men." He observed, that one member being asked, "What was their object, and whether they meant to seek "for any thing more than the repeal of the Corporation and "Test Acts?" answered, in the language of our Saviour, "We "know those things which ye are not yet able to bear." And when another member said, "Give them a little light into "what we intend," he informed him, that "they did not care "the nip of a straw for the repeal of those Acts; but that they "designed to try for the abolition of the Tythes, Liturgy, &c." To this unshaken Abdiel regard is due;

> His loyalty he kept, his love, his zeal;
> Nor number, nor example with him wrought
> To swerve from truth. MILTON.

low

low citizens: in the latter case, although the measure has been hitherto attended with no mischief, there is an overt-act against the public safety; for, by weakening the judgment, and inflaming the imagination, *these small pieces in vindication of liberty* are calculated to promote popular commotion, and to introduce disaffection and sedition amongst the multitude:

> Hac fonte derivata clades,
> In patriam populumque fluxit.

This specious artifice, which has been adopted by the associators in both instances, in order to cover their designs, and to carry their separate schemes into execution, is calculated to lull opposition asleep, and it may, for a while, impose upon the credulous. Thus, the insurgents in 1780 displayed the mock banners of religion and liberty, and numbers unwarily enlisted at the standard, unconscious of any intended evil: and the associators of the present times, copying the successful precedent, are the *declared asserters of the rights of men*, and the *avengers of their oppressed and persecuted fellow citizens*; and, improving on the model, they congratulate one another upon the daily incense offered at the shrine of Dissenting-Virtue: " We have received, with heart-felt satisfaction, " the testimonies of approbation with which our " conduct has been honoured *," &c. This tinsel

---

* See the Resolutions of a Meeting of the Committee, &c. held at the King's Head Tavern, Poultry, London, January 13th, 1790; Edward Jefferies, Esq; Chairman.

dress of *fancied* approbation has been put on to dazzle the understanding, and to confound the judgment, that the projected reformation of the state might not be exposed to scrutiny and defeat; and, as the design is of a deeper policy, a garb more tawdry and meretricious than usual was judged necessary;

> Lest an apprehension
> Should turn the tide of fearful faction,
> And breed a kind of question in their cause:
> For well they know, they of the offending side
> Must keep aloof from strict arbitrement,
> And stop all sight-holes, every loop, from whence
> The eye of reason may pry in upon them *.

It must be allowed then that these modern vindicators of liberty have arrayed themselves more gorgeously than their predecessors; but with singular negligence, whilst busied in attiring the frontispiece of faction, they have ludicrously exposed its nakedness in a less guarded quarter.

The indignation which, from *purity of conscience*, they have expressed against the impious policy of their country, in perverting sacred ordinances to civil purposes, must claim our *holy veneration*; on this popular subject their apologists are peculiarly eloquent: but, with inimitable assurance, they brand churchmen for their indelicacy in confounding religion with politics, at the very time that they are moulding their own ministers into vehicles

---

* Shakespear's Henry IV.

of faction, and prostituting the sanctity of their tabernacles to secular intrigue.

The Protestant Dissenters assembled at Warrington, after noticing the "*partiality, oppression,* and *injustice* of the Test laws, and commenting on the *injuries* that their country suffers by the exclusion of able and virtuous Dissenters from civil offices, declare, that they *cannot rest satisfied* whilst so gross a *violation of the rights of men* remains on our statute books: they therefore exhort their brethren, *as good citizens, to do all they can* to remove an obstacle which prevents the admission of *honest Dissenters* into public employments." And to impress these *honest* principles on the minds of the multitude, and excite their zeal for novelty, and laudable endeavours after reformation, they resolved, "That copies of these resolutions be sent to the ministers of the several congregations which are represented by their delegates in this meeting, accompanied with a request, *that they will publicly read them to their respective congregations* *."

Thus would they waken the spiritual repose of the low-roofed meeting-house into an appetence of temporalities, into a scramble for the perquisites of tide-waiting, and the lucre of an excise office †.

"These

---

* See the resolutions of a meeting of delegates from eight congregations of Protestant Dissenters, held at Warrington, January 6th, 1790.

† Persons of all ranks and degrees in the state, from the
gauge

"These things, indeed, they have articulated,
"Proclaimed at market crosses, read in churches,
"To face the garment of rebellion
"With some fair colour, that may please the eye
"Of fickle changelings, and poor discontents,
"Which gape and rub the elbow at the news
"Of hurly-burly innovation."

It will appear, upon further examination, that the pulpit has been, of late, the common vehicle of fanatical discontent. A spirit of prejudice against established laws, and an irreverence of government, has been industriously imparted, and the oratory has furnished out the fuel and materials of sedition.

An illustrious writer, whose skill in all the offices of civil life has not been equalled, points out to us the origin and progress of popular discontent. Sir Francis Bacon, treating of the cause and mischief of seditious insurrection, observes, that it originates in the murmurs and aversion of two parties, the higher orders in the state, and the commonalty: " When one of these is discontent, the danger is
" not great; for common people are of slow mo-
" tion, if they be not excited by the greater sort:
" and the greater sort are of small strength, except
" the multitude be apt and ready to move of them-
" selves. Then this is the danger, when the better
" sort *do but wait for the troubling of the waters*

gauge to the sceptre, are alike excluded from executive offices, except they receive the Sacrament according to the rites of the church of England.

" *amongst the meaner*, that then they may declare
themselves *."

It would be a very easy, although a tedious task, to point out passages and proofs from the sermons of several of the Dissenting ministers, of their attempts to instil into their respective audiences a distaste of all ordinances, civil and religious. The conventicle has resounded with ideal tyranny, and fanatic reformation, and the press has teemed with fables of iron-handed persecution, and with predictions of a golden age of liberty. Trope has followed trope, and metaphor urged on metaphor, to animate the easy, inglorious sectary to deeds of pious anarchy; the Tests, the Church, the Supremacy are no humble objects; and when Kings, Laws, and Bishops are the promised plunder, what *friend to Liberty* would tamely rest in the *weak piping time of peace?*

Hinc concussa *fides*, et multis utile bellum.

How far their doctrine has spread contagion within the limits of the meeting-house, I am unwilling to enquire; but if their religio-political directory has been as favourably received without, which they insinuate, as it has been fervidly enforced within the pale of dissension; it is high time some antidote should be administered to correct the malignant influence. This they have abundantly furnished; for a naked exhibition of

* Sir F. Bacon's Essays.

the real principles of this *gospel-preaching ministry*, stripped of their borrowed frippery, will be sufficient to convince their deluded followers, that " though their voice be Jacob's voice, yet their " hands are the hands of Esau."

It would be wasting too much of my time, and it would weary the patience of my reader, was I to quote the multitude of inflammatory and libellous publications, which have issued from the overheated brains of those usurping sons of Levi, who *have of late taken so much upon them, murmuring alike against the priesthood, and the rulers of the people.* I shall only notice the zealous deeds of two, who are leaders *in the assembly, famous in the congregation, men of renown:* Who, in fomenting schism in the church, and dissension in the state, have misapplied talents, that would have adorned society, and might have rendered real services to mankind.

These holy champions of revolt,

—— " whose virtues would be proud
" If their faults whipp'd them not: and whose crimes
" Would despair, if they were not cherished by their virtues:

These reverend abettors of sedition, are not content to *wait for the troubling of the waters*, but improvidently agitate the fearful element; and, instead of inspiring their people with the spirit of truth, unity, and concord, they have mingled the perverse spirit of discord and dissension, with the spirit of promise and the spirit of prophecy. " What " we are aiming at is to *enlighten the minds of the* " *people,*

"*people*, and to shew them that, in the Church
" Establishment of this country, there is much of
" error and superstition: and if we can convince
" them that it is so (and of this I have no doubt)
" in proper time *they will take it down themselves.*"
See Letter to the Right honourable William Pitt,
1787, by Jos. Priestley, LL.D.

" The enemies of reformation do not suffici-
" ently consider, that, by opposing, in enlightened
" times, all attempts to remove such *shocking ble-*
" *mishes* from our established code of faith and
" worship, they expose the hierarchy to particular
" danger of a *sudden and total overthrow*. As a
" friend to the free progress of truth, and an enemy
" to all *slavish hierarchies, I could almost wish they*
" *may persevere in their obstinacy.*" Sermons on the
Christian Doctrine, by Richard Price, D. D. &c.
1787.

" If you *must* have a state religion (for which I
" own I see no occasion whatever) let it be at least
" something *rational and intelligible*; something that
" mankind may see to afford a *natural* foundation
" of good conduct here, and of reasonable expec-
" tation hereafter: and such is the Unitarian doc-
" trine *." Letter to the Right honourable William
Pitt, by Joseph Priestley, LL. D. &c.

" Happy

---

* I cannot help noticing in this place a droll coincidence of project; that wicked rogue Tom Woolston, in the true spirit of badinage, proposed to give up Christianity, and *solemnly* recommended his " golden religion of nature " in its stead. See Woolst. Disc. vi. p. 28.

"Happy will the world be, when *these truths*
"shall be every where acknowledged and practised
"upon. Religious bigotry, that cruel demon, will
"be then laid asleep; *slavish governments* and *slavish*
"*hierarchies* will then sink." "So injurious are
"civil establishments of formularies of faith and
"worship, that it has long been a subject of dispute,
"which is worst in its effects on society, *such* a re-
"ligion, or *speculative Atheism*. *For my own part,*
"*I could almost give the preference to the latter.*"
Observations on the Importance of the American
Revolution, by Richard Price, D. D. LL. D.

"If we be successful in the *propagation of the*
"*truth*, we need not give ourselves *any concern about*
"*the measures of government* concerning it. Causes
"will always produce their effects; and, though the
"cases be of a different nature, it is as certain an
"inference as any in geometry, that an *Unitarian*
"*people cannot long be subject to a Trinitarian establish-*
"*ment*. Things are already in such a train, that,
"though no person can foresee the particular time

Woolston, however, was not chargeable with the *furor innovantium*. This arch-disputant well knew that there was an insuperable obstacle to any *serious* proposal of the kind; he was aware "that every king and queen at their coronation were "obliged to take and subscribe *an oath to preserve the settlement* "*of the Church of England, and the doctrine, discipline, and go-* "*vernment* thereof, within the kingdoms of England and Ire- "land, and the territories thereunto belonging; and that this "Act (5 Ann. c. 5.) should be held a fundamental and essential "part of the Union betwixt the two kingdoms of England and "Scotland."

"and manner of the change in favour of Unitarianism, we may be as certain of its taking place,
as if we saw it actually accomplished." See
Sermon on the Importance and Extent of Free Enquiry, &c. by Jof. Priestley, LL. D.

"Religious improvement must be expected to
keep pace with other improvements. It is observable that the scriptures place the *downfall of
antichrist* before the commencement of the universal kingdom of the Messiah. Previously to
this, it must lose that connection with civil power
which has debased it, and which now, in almost
every Christian country, turns it into a scheme of
worldly emolument and policy, and supports
error and superstition under the name of it. The
absurdities fathered upon it must be exploded," &c. See Sermon in the Old Jewry Meeting-house, London, April 1787, by Richard Price, D. D.

"Assure yourself, Sir, that the Unitarian doctrine has already taken deep root in the church
itself; and it is a plant of a strong constitution,
and makes vigorous shoots. The present controversy greatly quickens its growth; and, in spite
of all the efforts of churchmen, and of all that as
a statesman you can do to assist them, the doctrines which constitute the peculiar faith of the
church of England *must fall before it*; and, if the
hierarchy will obstinately maintain these doctrines,
and keep up the subscription to them, it must in
time fall with them." Letter to the Right Hon.
William Pitt, by Joseph Priestley, LL. D.

"The

" The late (American) war did great good by disseminating just sentiments of the rights of mankind, and the nature of legitimate government.—But in its termination, the war has done still greater good, by preserving the new governments from that destruction in which they must have been involved, *had Britain conquered:* by providing, in a sequestered continent, a place of refuge for opprest men in every region of the world; and by laying the foundation there of an empire which may be the seat of liberty, science, and virtue, and from whence there is reason to hope these sacred blessings will spread till they become universal, *and the time arrives when kings and priests shall have no more power to oppress, and that ignominious slavery, which has hitherto debased the world, is exterminated.*" Observations on the Importance of the American Revolution, by Richard Price, D. D. LL.D. F.R.S.

It is unnecessary to multiply instances, from the various publications of these patrons of novelty, of their aversion from regular government; but, in justice to them, I should observe, that they have been sensible of their injudicious conduct, and in some late sober expositions have attempted to appease the censure of men and the vengeance of the laws[*]. Their apologists

---

[*] The reverend author of the " Observations on the Importance of the American Revolution," honestly acknowledges, that, in consequence of *the warm part* he had taken in the rebellion of the British colonies, he had exposed himself to *much* abuse, and to *some danger* from the violated laws of his country.

apologists, too have been busy in glossing over their indecent labours; have opposed to the charge of faction, *the force, the nerve, the beauty of metaphor*; and have qualified the *principles* of rebellion, by attributing *to honest zeal its wonted imprudence, but upright intentions.* But what opinion can we have of that cause, or of its advocates, who are either involved in a train of indiscretions, or engaged in a tissue of apologies? Will the ample cloak of reformation cover all the sins of restless zeal? or will unblushing revolutionists veil over every unsightly excrescence? In defiance of those important and puzzling apothegms, " That an " independent parliament is incompatible with the " existence of the monarchy;" and, " That a " church polity, conformable to the genius of the " civil constitution, is indispensably necessary to na- " tional religion ;" we have a flaming patriot declaring from the rostrum, that he has worked himself up beyond his strength, and is well nigh exhausted, at the glorious prospect of " establishing

---

This gentleman, in some later editions of his sermons, particularly of his popular discourse on the love of our country, November 1789, has thought it prudent to soften down some offensive strokes of oratory. This has been judged a necessary practice by Dr. Priestley, and particularly in his sermon at Birmingham, on the conduct to be observed by the Dissenters upon the eve of their application to parliament; in which he has atoned for former inflammatory expressions, in some degree, by a calm and rational eloquence. And it pains one to observe an untimely hint, " That more relaxations are intended than have been " as yet solicited."

" theism

"theism on the ruins of the episcopal hierarchy, and the *independence of the three states of* the British government on one another, in which its essence consists *." Yet, a little after, we hear the same divine, in the same sanctuary, forgetful of former political speculations, affirming with gross inconsistency, that the monarchy is essentially *dependent*, and the king a mere creature of the public. "A king is *no more* than the first servant of the public, created by it, maintained by it, and responsible to it: and all the homage paid him, is due to him *on no other account* than the community. His sacredness is the sacredness of the community: his authority is the authority of the community: and the term Majesty, which it is usual to apply to him, is *by no means* his own majesty, but the majesty of the people †." I forbear commenting on the indecency of handling this subject in the pulpit, and the tendency of such doctrine to inflame the conventicle. But I must ask these delegates of evangelical peace, whether they are in actual possession of their consciences, when they thus prostitute the dignity of the laws, the honour of the crown,

---

* See a Discourse on the Evidence of a future Period of Improvement, with the *means* and *duty* of promoting it, delivered at the O'd Jewry Meeting-house, April 25, 1787, before the *supporters of a new academical institution*, by Richard Price, D.D. F.R.S. &c.

† See a Discourse on the Love of our Country, delivered at the Old Jewry Meeting-house, November 1789, by Richard Price, D.D. F.R.S. &c.

the rights of the church, and the privileges of parliament, to the visionary liberties of the people, to be trampled on by overheated sectaries,

> Ignavum pecus, quod a præsepibus arcent?

Experience has long since convinced us of the fatal consequences that have flowed from this rant for liberty and the rights of conscience: but when politics supersede piety, and zeal takes place of order,

> " 'Tis too much prov'd, that with devotion's visage,
> " And pious action, men do sugar o'er
> " The devil himself."

I hope I shall not wound the feelings of these reverent votaries of privilege, when I tell them that they greatly overrate this majesty of the people, and that the rights and liberties of the subject may be urged too far, and become, even in these *enlightened days*, as necessarily to be resisted, especially on the *eve of innovation*, as ever prerogative was in the last century: because " political innovations commonly
" produce many effects besides those that are in-
" tended. The direct consequence is often the least
" important. Incidental, remote, and unthought-
" of evils or advantages frequently exceed the good
" that is designed, or the inconveniency that is fore-
" seen *." Far be it from me to intrench upon the rights of man, or the dignity of human nature, or

* See Archdeacon Paley's Principles of Moral and Political Philosophy, p. 467.

what has of late been called the majesty of the people, from whom the chief magistrate originally derives his power, and to whom he affords by a reciprocal tie his protection. The absolute rights and civil liberties of Englishmen are clearly defined; they have the security of person and property; the right of self-defence; the constitution and power of parliaments; and the limitation of royal prerogative; the regular administration of justice, and the right of petitioning for redress of grievances. These are their rights, whether as individuals, or members of the community: and as to any other popular privilege, undefined by the municipal laws, the constitution acknowledges none; but, on the contrary, has restrained the *natural liberty* of mankind by laws that are absolutely necessary for the preservation of society.

But there is a rock on which republicans in a monarchical government are generally apt to split. They lift up the dignity of the people, and misinterpret and depress the royal authority, and, reducing the chief magistrate to the condition of a servant, insinuating that his power is merely delegated, and reassumable at will, they effectually destroy the very essence of a monarchical constitution. Is our celebrated revolutionist yet to learn, that the king's prerogative is independent of the people; that his crown descends to him by the positive constitution of the kingdom; and, notwithstanding parliamentary limitations, the crown retains its descendible quality, and is hereditary in the prince to whom it is limited:

mited: and if he maintains the contract betwixt himself and his people, which is expressed in his coronation oath, and is founded in the very nature of society; that is, if the king governs his people according to the laws, and *maintains the established religion of his country*, he is *then* entitled to our reverence and allegiance, not merely as the *first servant of the public*, but as possessing the constitutional and legal attributes of *personal sovereignty, absolute perfection, and political perpetuity?* Is the champion of *rights* yet to learn, that, for the preservation of this monarchy, and the maintenance of the regal dignity, *adherence to the king's enemies* is punishable as high treason *; *and contempt of his person and government*, is subject to *fine and imprisonment* †: that, for the defence of religion, and the security of the public peace, *reviling the established ordinances* ‡, *tumultuous petitioning* §, *pretended prophecies and libels* ‖, are all restrained by forfeiture, imprisonment, and infamous corporal punishment?

There is in some men an innate principle of opposition to those whose province it is to reprove, to restrain, and to rebuke; and, whatever the *friends* of such men may think of their multiplied indiscre-

---

* By the statute of Edward III.

† By speaking or writing contemptuously, &c. see 4th Ann. c. 8. and 6th Ann. c. 7.

‡ Seditious words, spoken in derogation of the established religion, are indictable, *as tending to a breach of the peace.* See 1 Haw. 7. and 1 Eliz. c. 2. § 4.

§ By the 13th Charles II. c. 1. and 1st George, c. 5.

‖ See 5th Eliz. c. 15. and 3 Inst. 128 and 129.

tions,

tions, *their enemies* will be apt to impute their difguft of ordinances, to a dread of infulted authority, and their cry for liberty, to the apprehenfions of a prifon.

But I may be told that our reverend politician has avowed himfelf an enemy to commonwealths, and an advocate for monarchy. I know this: and he has done more. With wonderful verfatility of talent, he has difowned profelytifm, and retained the fpirit and zeal for converfion*; has abandoned controverfy, in the midft of polemical pofitions †; and, fheltering himfelf behind fome equivocal axiom of the celebrated Montefquieu, has condemned democracy, and difleminated republican principles ‡.

A character

---

* Compare " Sermons on the Chriftian Doctrine, as received " by the different Denominations of Chriftians," by R. Price; and his " Difcourfe on the Evidence of a future Period of Improvement;" with " Obfervations on the American Revolution," by Richard Price, D.D. paffim.

† In the advertifement prefixed to Dr. Price's " Sermons " on the Chriftian Doctrine," he declares his refolution not to engage in controverfy; yet in the body of the fame work, he not only charges churchmen with *idolatry*, but enters into a curious comparifon of the Athanafian and Socinian fyftems, declaring, that in regard to the *Deity of Chrift*, " as far as Trini" tarians and Socinians have ideas, they are agreed on this " fubject; and the war they have been maintaining againft one " another, has been entirely a war of words."

‡ In his " Difcourfe on the Evidence of a future Period of " Improvement," the Doctor expreffly difclaims republican principles; and has gone fo far as to acknowledge that our conftitution of government is better adapted to this country

than

A character so paradoxical, we are led to think, could neither be the favourite of a party, nor the idol of the tabernacle, now prostituted to *civil dudgeon* and *phrenetic mood*; and we might reasonably expect that diffidents would no longer impute iniquity to establishments of faith,

> "———— when their own bishop
> "Turns insurrection to religion;
> "Supposed sincere and holy in his thoughts,
> "Derives from Heaven his quarrel and his cause.
> "Tells them he doth bestride a bleeding land
> "Gasping for life.————
> "And more, or less, do flock to follow him."

But this age is the age of *experiment*: the principles of *civil dissolution* and political augury are transmitted and imbibed with theological precepts; and speculative saints have arrived at the temple of fame, through the eccentric paths of *state chemistry* and *divination*: nay, to prove the utmost powers of combination, a projector has been found to re-

---

than any other: yet, in most other publications, particularly in his late Sermon "On the Love of our Country," he entirely depreciates the regal authority, and condemns all interposition of civil power in matters of religion: and in his "Observations " on the Importance of the American Revolution," he glories in the emancipation of our late fellow-subjects from regal tyranny, and, kindling with a zeal for reformation, he fervently petitions Heaven " *to put a speedy end to all creed establishments* " *of religion!*" unmindful that the great charter has *inseparably* woven the establishment into the civil constitution; and that the monarchy can stand no longer than the *doctrine, discipline, and present government* of the Church of England is maintained. See 12th W. III. c. 2. and 5th Ann. c. 5.

commend

commend the abasers of monarchy, and the declared foes of church establishments, *as well qualified* to fill the offices of a regal and episcopal government*.

I shall now take leave of these gentlemen for a season; but, as we may meet again, I think it proper to assure them, that in my strictures on their principles, I gratify no personal enmity; their zeal for *godly-thorough reformation*, as far as it has operated on their conduct as subjects and as citizens, is a fair object of animadversion: and, though they have offended against the rules of decency and good order, and have violated the laws of their country, by wounding her constitution, and assailing the best interests of her religion, through the medium of *her own press*, it is my sincere wish that they may never be overtaken by popular insult, or personal injury.—Errors in politics, as well as in divinity, should be treated with the same correctives as errors in ethics or philosophy: prejudice should be subdued by reason, and opinions should be condemned, not by the powers of magistracy, but upon the detection of sophism and fallacy; and religious as well as political orthodoxy may be well supported without an arm of flesh; for upon sound argument and fair discussion, truth will always obtain the

---

* Mr. Fox, in the debate upon the repeal of the Tests, March 3d 1790, noticed the writings of Dr. Price against the hierarchy; but he insisted that there would be no more danger to the constitution, in admitting him to any office in the state, than there was in permitting the Chancellor of the Exchequer, who objected to the present representation of the people in parliament, to be at the head of the treasury.

victory. But it by no means follows, that legal reftrictions are either impolitic, unneceffary, or unjuft; and, although nothing is to be dreaded from controverfy, except when giving rife to tumult and commotion, yet there have been occafions when the public fecurity has depended on the very laws that are now fo obnoxious, and to which indeed we are indebted for our prefent enjoyment of civil and religious liberty: and, however the principles of humanity and benevolence fhould reftrain the execution of penal laws in matters of opinion, yet the common policy of prevention will teach a well-conftituted ftate to preferve certain barriers betwixt liberty and licentioufnefs. " Oh, 'tis excellent to " have a giant's ftrength, but, it is tyrannous to ufe " it like a giant!"—Shakefpear.

It is a ftale and common practice with innovators, to impute to the advocates for eftablifhments and regular government, an adherence to High-Church principles and prerogative: but let me afk that man, who is unbiaffed by education, by religious prejudice or connection, whether, in the prefent times, more mifchief is not to be apprehended from a clamour for abftract rights, and a zeal for reformation, than from any undue influence of prerogative, or any ambitious defigns of churchmen? We have a monarch who has inflexibly purfued a juft, equitable, and confiftent conduct, who has confidered his own intereft as interwoven with the welfare of his fubjects, and whofe happinefs has confifted in promoting the profperity of

his

his people: we have a religion, I speak of it as an establishment, that disowns persecution, and abhors every measure subversive of liberty, and which, through the blessed spirit of toleration, is the very prop and support of social happiness. Our clergy, as a collective body, are equally distinguished for their learning, mildness, and liberality, as they are for their abhorrence of profligacy and libertinism. A pure administration of justice prevails amongst us, as pure at least as the state of things here will admit of. Our judges are incorrupt; questions of right and wrong are justly decided; and the interests of the individual are preserved from the griping hands of the oppressor. A tide of wealth and prosperity is flowing in upon us; the affections of a grateful people are secured by mild, equal, and beneficial laws; whilst national honour is maintained abroad in unusual splendour. Such is the spirit and the effect of our happy constitution. As free subjects of a free government, we may cherish our allegiance without betraying ourselves into servitude, and we may exercise our freedom, without owing any *vassalage*, except to those laws which are of our own prescribing. The efforts of faction and ambition may indeed excite a feeble murmur, and promote a partial discontent; but an enlightened people cannot be long deluded by false reasoning and false patriotism. "The voice of joy and gladness shall put to silence the voice of him that reproacheth;" and a just tribute of applause shall be paid to those who are to perpetuate these blessings to us, with the ardour of British gratitude, and in the spirit of Roman approbation. "Quapropter, de summâ salute nostrâ, patres conscripti, de conjugibus ac liberis, de aris et focis, de fanis ac templis, de totius urbis tectis ac sedibus, de imperio, de libertate, de salute patriæ, deque universâ republicâ decernite diligenter, ut instituistis, ac fortiter *."

I now resume my comparison of the conduct of the Protestant Dissenters in 1789, with that of the Protestant Associators in 1780.

Another measure adopted by the insurgents in 1780, in *vindication of liberty,* has been in no small degree copied by the present associated body of Dissenters. I mean the attempt to obtain an alteration of the established laws, by *overawing the legislature.* The proceedings in each case are not exactly alike, but the tendency was the same, and equally unconstitutional. In the first instance, the danger to the constitution was not so imminent as the outrage on the persons of the senators was offensive. The tumultuous petitioning of the *bellua*

* " Wherefore, senators, go on as you have begun, with diligence and resolution, to provide for the public safety, and that of our wives and children, for our temples and altars, the city and its buildings, the empire, the liberty and welfare of our country, and for the good of the whole commonwealth."
CICERO.

centiceps

centiceps will generally defeat its own intentions; and in this case, the firmness and intrepidity with which parliament resisted the daring violation of its freedom and privilege, contributed alike to the preservation of the laws and the maintenance of its dignity. But now the representatives of the people are to be assailed less hostilely indeed, but more insidiously; not with open acts of violence, but with the covert evils of stratagem and intrigue. " And covert evils are generally more dangerous " to all governments than those which are appa- " rent, and capable of exciting immediate alarm *." In either case, the desertion of their constitutional duties was the object; in the former, by a daring outrage on the persons of the senators and the freedom of debate; in the latter, by a deliberate and artful attack on their integrity and independence; by a censure on such as had opposed their repeated applications for a repeal of the Tests, and by a solemn declaration to return such only, at the next general election, as would pledge themselves to support the private interests of a party. And, however offensive the conduct of the associators in 1780 might be, I have no hesitation in saying, that the measures of the associators in 1789 were pregnant with greater mischief to the constitution. As this charge is of a serious nature, it must be treated with attention, and if it is not established on fact, the

---

* See Rights of the Protestant Dissenters asserted, &c. part 2. c. 5.

accuser must be overwhelmed in the obloquy deservedly due to calumniators. Dismissing then for a while, the first tribe of insurgents, we are to inquire how far the conduct of the present Associated Dissenters tends to overawe and influence the legislature. It is a fundamental principle in the constitution of this country, " That elections should " be free, and the elected independent." In direct violation of this salutary maxim, the Protestant Dissenters have concerted plans, which in their operation strike directly at the freedom of election, and the independence of the representative.

Having formed confederacies throughout the kingdom, with a view to the repeal of those ancient tests, which the *majority* of their fellow-citizens have always considered and repeatedly declared to be the great security and defence of the crown, and the permanency of the British constitution; and judging that their intended application would meet with little redress from that parliament, which after mature discussion had already twice solemnly declared against it, they look forward to the period of its dissolution, and violently strain every nerve to effect the return of a better-tempered legislature. At the season then of a general election, a season at all times of faction and division, when the minds of men are agitated by contending interests, and the little weaknesses that are too often found amongst the best, float uppermost; in this hour of mental infirmity, the unblushing advocates of civil and religious

ligious liberty press forward, and urge *a test* * on those very men who are to thunder for them in the senate, in behalf of *abstract rights and natural privilege*, in support of *absolute liberty, just and true liberty, equal and impartial liberty* †. This palpable absurdity would not be credited on my bare assertion: I am necessitated therefore to adduce other proof in confirmation of the fact; and it is nothing less than the *cool deliberate resolution* of a body of Protestant Dissenters, assembled at Bolton in Lancashire ‡. " It is highly expedient and proper for
" all Dissenting freeholders and electors through-
" out the kingdom, in every county, city, and bo-
" rough, to require by letter, of all candidates for
" a seat in parliament, with whom they are seve-
" rally concerned, an *explicit declaration* of their
" views respecting the Test and Corporation Acts,
" and *to refuse their votes to every man who will not
" engage* to support a repeal of acts which *appear
" to be* obnoxious, intolerant, and unjust: *and of all
" penal statutes against religious principles*."

Here is a resolution as eminent for zeal, as it is

---

* This argument was most happily urged by the Chancellor of the Exchequer, in the debate on Mr. Fox's motion, March 3d, 1790; and it was, although on a dissimilar occasion, touched upon with pointed application by a former minister: " It does " not become those who will not observe covenants or treaties, " to press them upon others." Sir Thomas Bodley's speech to the Dutch, in the reign of Queen Elizabeth.

† See Right of Protestant Dissenters, &c. asserted, p. 50. note; and preface to the first edition of the Confessional.

‡ December 17th, 1789.

for absurdity, and which holds forth a ridiculous mixture of latitude and intolerance!

In a free country every thing is to be apprehended from an undue exertion of privilege, and to delude or entrap the representatives of the people by influence and stratagem, is ungenerous and unconstitutional. If the Dissenters were the only persons concerned in the repeal of the established Tests, even then their plea for a redress of grievances should not pass without a strict examination, because the means which they have made use of to carry their point have excited suspicion; but when, under the pretext of religion and liberty, the very existence of that establishment for which we have been so long contending, is attacked, the cool deliberate resolution to influence the freedom of election, and to ensnare the judgment of that man who is to be the representative, not of the Dissenters only, but of every member in the community, rouses the attention of every one who is not indifferent to his real interests; for the subject comes home to him, and his conscience and reason must tell him, in spite of fine-spun arguments, that the conduct of these men is *not to be justified in this particular*, by any pretext of personal inconvenience, or claim for private emolument.

But these men assure us they are *good citizens, friends to civil liberty, friends to the establishments in church and state*, and that they are only adopting *some constitutional measures to effect their desireable purpose*. When their plaintive brethren aimed at the repeal of the offensive statutes in 1780, they exhibited a juster knowledge of the British constitution, and betrayed a jealousy of the honour of their senators, unknown to the associators of 1789. They expressed, in their petition to parliament, an apprehension, lest the Roman Catholics, by the indulgence recently granted to them, "*should influence* " *our elections in future parliaments, which would* " *tend to the destruction of our happy constitution* *." They too, but a few hours before they subverted the civil power, and ere

> " The burning ruins with a fiercer ray
> " Supply'd the sun, and counterfeited day:"

They too, in the very act of overawing parliament, were *good citizens, friends to civil liberty, and the establishments in church and state.* " Your petitioners " presume, that their peaceable deportment, and " the *constitutional steps* they have taken to obtain " redress, will meet with the *approbation* of this " honourable house *." There is an animation in Roman politics that captivates while it convinces: " An tu populum Romanum esse illum putas qui " constat ex iis, qui mercede conducuntur? qui " impelluntur, ut vim afferant Magistratibus? ut " obsideant senatum? cui populo duces Lentidios, " Lollios, Sergios, præfeceras. O speciem, digni-

* See the petition of Protestant Associators, presented by lord G. Gordon, at the bar of the House of Commons, June 2d, 1780, signed by 40,000; and said to be brought up by 100,000 *vindicators of liberty.*

" tatemque

" tatemque populi Romani, quam reges, quam na-
" tiones exteræ, quam gentes ultimæ pertimefcunt;
" multitudinem hominum ex fervis conductis, ex
" facinorofis, ex egentibus congregatam."—Cicero.

The text may be eafily applied, I leave it to others to interpret; but there needs no commentary.

But I turn from thefe unjuftifiable meafures to an object that claims peculiar attention. A pamphlet, anonymous indeed, comes forward to the public with fingular commendation. The author profeffes " to give an accurate narrative of facts, and to " ftate the principles on which the Proteftant Dif- " fenters found their claim to a complete tolera- " tion." And he has been ufhered into public notice under the fanction of a noble earl*, and the applaufes of a diftinguifhed commoner †. The firft commends this pamphlet as the beft that has been publifhed *upon religion*, for a whole century; the laft applauds it as a moft accurate and fair ftatement of the Diffenters rights; and it has obtained equal commendation from authority ‡ much
higher

---

* Earl Stanhope.
† Sir H. Hophton. See Debates, March 3d, 1790.
‡ " The narrative part of this piece ftates fully, and we think
" fairly, the Hiftory of the Teft laws: the argumentative part
" reafons clearly and forcibly on the injuftice and impolicy of
" excluding from public offices a part of the community, who,
" &c. &c. The facts and argument, ftated in this publication, fo
" decifively eftablifh the expediency as well as the juftice of the
" repeal

higher in the court of criticifm. A publication fo favourably announced awakens curiofity and attracts attention, and it fhould contain important, accurate, and impartial intelligence *. The importance of this pamphlet to the interefts of religion, and the correctnefs and fidelity of its hiftorical references, may be the fubject of future invefligation; at prefent I am to examine whether it is calculated to promote undue influence, and to affect the freedom of elec-

" repeal of the Teft Acts, that we cannot fuppofe that it will be
" long in the power of the obfolete cry, *The church is in danger*,
" to prevent it." Month. Rev. vol. lxxx. p. 561.

* The author of " The Right of the Proteftant Diffenters to
" a complete Toleration afferted," informs us, in his preface, that he was employed but little more *than fix weeks* in *writing and publifhing* the firft edition of his work: an intimation that implies either negligence and hurry, or fuperiority of abilities. As the fubject is very important, and comprehends not only the defigns of the Diffenters, but the welfare of the eftablifhed religion, we may fairly conclude that this Treatife, on which fo little time has been beftowed, will neither ftand the teft of examination, nor obtain diftinction for accuracy and fidelity: confcious of deficiency, the writer refers us to a publication of the Reverend Mr. Fownes, of Shrewfbury, intitled, " An Inquiry " into the Principles of Toleration." The work of this refpectable minifter has not as yet come within my notice; but, to this fortrefs and rock of refuge for Diffenting principles, I fhall turn with eagernefs, in expectation of finding found argument and fair deduction. In the mean time, I fhall remark, that precipitation in a matter fo complicated and involved, inevitably incurs that cenfure which is deftined to fallacious facts, fophiftical inferences, and flimfy argument. And, whatever the friends of this afferter of rights may think, his abilities, however tranfcendent, will not fecure that reputation of which his negligence and artifice have bereaved him.

tion, and the independence of the elected. And here, if I might hazard a conjecture, it appears, that from this approved model, this *prototype of reformation*, the Protestant Dissenters have framed their late resolutions and proceedings.

This writer, after having bestowed a plentiful share of censure on the whole bench of bishops, as " supporters of tenets in public, which in private " they utterly disclaim," sums up the credenda et agenda of Religious Dissension in this animated peroration. " Let not the Protestant Dissenters
" put their trust in king, minister, or prelates; but
" let them *confide in their own exertions*, the justice
" of their cause, and the generosity of the nation.
" Let them not be withheld by promises, or inti-
" midated by threats, from prosecuting their design,
" or *using all the helps which Providence has placed*
" *in their power*. There is not an individual among
" them, however humble his situation, however
" confined his sphere of action, who may not exert
" himself with effect. By conversation with his
" neighbours, by correspondence with his friends,
" he may conciliate our enemies, and make the
" lukewarm zealous. Besides, the time cannot be
" far remote, when the representatives of the peo-
" ple must give an account of their trust to their
" constituents; and that power which the Dissenters
" so signally displayed at the dissolution of the last
" parliament, must have considerable influence at
" the conclusion of the present. Such a crisis in
" favour of the Dissenters may not occur in the re-
" volution

"volution of ages; *and it is a duty to themselves*
"*and their posterity to take advantage of it.* They
" are peculiarly the guardians of religious liberty,
" and will shortly have an opportunity to shew
" their attachment to its friends. Those who shall
" have approved their regard for the rights of con-
" science, and voted for the repeal of the Tests,
" may go down with confidence to their consti-
" tuents, who are *Dissenters, and friends of religious*
" *liberty*; while the *obstinate advocates for persecution*
" *can have no claim to their assistance*.*"

This is the Catholic creed of Protestant Dissen-sion; and, without a question, the damnatory clauses favour strongly of political Calvinism. But is the eve of the dissolution of parliament to be the eve of the violation of senatorial privilege? Is the suffrage of the candidate to be pre-engaged to support an unknown system of reformation? his faith pledged to personal interests, or his reluctance to make shipwreck of parliamentary virtue, wounded by personal resentment? Yet so it is! And I have lived to see the day, when the representative of a free people is to be intimidated into compliance with party views, or branded as *an obstinate advocate for persecution!*

Every elector is in possession of civil privileges and constitutional rights; and if he is wise, he will delegate them as pure as he has received them; and when in the act of surrendering his most valu-

---

* Right of the Protestant Dissenters to a complete Toleration asserted, p. 97.

able interests, his liberty, to the guardianship of another, he will take care not to accompany it with a fetter. A combination of men may declaim upon their rights to dictate to their candidate; but that man must have more than Machiavelian craft and ingenuity to persuade me, that this boasted right is *an active power* to hamper the freedom of others, or to invade the privileges of their fellow-citizens. In short, however I may abhor the insults offered to the legislature by the associators in 1780, I have no hesitation in saying, that a cool premeditated attack on the freedom of election, and on the delicacy, the honour, and independence of a British senator, is full as alarming to the general interests of the public, as an outrage committed on the person of majesty itself.

But we are told that this measure has a precedent: " That power which the Dissenters so sig-
" nally displayed at the dissolution of the last par-
" liament, must have considerable influence at the
" conclusion of the present." And will precedent sanction what is inconsistent with reason and sound policy? So thought faction of old. " *Vivimus ad*
" *exempla, nec ratione componimur, sed consuetudine*
" *abducimur.*" It is true this measure has a precedent; a precedent indeed of the same complexion, but of a very different date from that alluded to. And as it applies in many instances to the subject under discussion; I shall be excused, even by the Dissenters themselves, for quoting it in the words of Burnet. The bishop, after remark-
ing

ing on the infidious views of the Popish monarch James II. in setting out his declaration for toleration and liberty of conscience in 1687, proceeds, "This gave great offence to all true patriots, as well as to the whole church-party. The preamble, that pretended so much love and charity, and that condemned persecution, founded strangely in the mouth of a Popish prince. Upon this, a new set of addresses went round the Dissenters. And they who had so long reproached the Church of England, as too courtly in their submissions and flatteries, seemed now to vie with them in those abject strains. They magnified the king's mercy and favour, and made great protestations of fidelity and gratitude. Many promised to endeavour, *that such persons should be chosen to serve in parliament, as should concur with the king in the enacting what he now granted so graciously.* The king and his priests were delighted with these addresses out of measure: and they seemed to think that they had gained the nation, and had now conquered those who were hitherto their most irreconcileable enemies. But seeing no hope of prevailing on his parliament (to concur with him in his aims at arbitrary power) he dissolved it; but gave it out, that he would have a new one before winter; and soon after set out on a progress through some of the western counties. In the places through which he passed, the king saw a visible coldness both in the nobility and

"gentry,

" gentry. On his part, he was very obliging to all
" that came near him, and moſt particularly to the
" *Diſſenters*, and to thoſe who had paſſed long
" under *the notion of commonwealth's men*. He ran
" out on the points of liberty of conſcience. He was
" well pleaſed to hear all the ill-natured ſtories that
" were brought him of the violences committed
" of late, either by the juſtices of peace, or by the
" clergy. *He every where* recommended to them
" the chooſing ſuch parliament-men as would con-
" cur with him in ſettling *this liberty* as firmly as
" the Magna Charta had been: and to this he
" never forgot to add, *the taking away the Teſts*.
" Many books were now writ for liberty of con-
" ſcience; *and, ſince all people ſaw what ſecurity the*
" *Teſts gave*, theſe ſpoke of an equivalent to be
" offered, that ſhould give a further ſecurity, beyond
" what could be pretended from the Teſts."—The
king was making every day a very arbitrary uſe
of the power of changing the magiſtracy. The
regulators, who aſſiſted him in this work, " were
" for the moſt part Diſſenters gained by the court,
" and they went on very boldly, and turned men
" out upon every ſtory that was made of them;
" and put ſuch men in their room as they confided
" in. After this, the king ſent orders to the lords
" lieutenants of the counties to examine the gentle-
" men and freeholders upon three queſtions: the
" firſt was, Whether, in caſe they ſhould be choſen
" to ſerve in parliament, they would conſent to
" repeal

RELIGIOUS DISSENSION.

"repeal the penal laws, and those for the Tests?
"the second was, Whether they would give their
"vote for choosing such men as would engage to
"do that? And the third was, Whether they would
"maintain the king's declaration?—In most of the
"counties, the lords lieutenants put those questions
"in so careless a manner, that it was plain they did
"not desire they should be answered in the affir-
"mative. Some went further, and declared them-
"selves against them. And a few of the more re-
"solute refused to put them. They said, this was
"*the prelimiting and the packing a parliament, which*
"*in its nature was to be free, and under no previous*
"*engagement* *."

Here is a coalition indeed! a coalition of Popery and Dissension in support of religious freedom! The eve of the dissolution of Parliament is the season

"For party-saint to slip his fetter." HUD.

And Popery winks, whilst Dissension seeks her spiritual enlargement amidst the cabals of a canvass, and the riots of an election.

* Burnet's History of his own Times.

I dismiss the subject, and shall now take leave of my reader; and if these few observations on the principles and conduct of the Protestant Dissenters shall have attracted his attention, it remains with him to consider what inferences and what use may be drawn from them. He must remark, that, although there are many upright and pious men who dissent from the established Church, there is no reason to suppose that these are adherents to the present system of reformation. He must recollect, from the instances adduced, that the appeal of the Dissenters to history, in proof of their patriotism and political virtue, serves only to condemn their principles and their actions;—that their specious vindication of civil and religious liberty has been the stale trick of reformers in all ages, *ad captandum vulgus*, calculated only for the fickle and unwary; —that their censure on the Establishment, for confounding religion with politics, recoils with tenfold accusation on their own heads;—that their pretended disgust of Tests, when they are forging fetters for those who are the peculiar guardians of liberty, is a gross absurdity;—that their determination to renew their attack on the established laws of their country, *at every favourable opportunity*, menaces the public security, and destroys all confidence in them as citizens and subjects. In short—that their eagerness to promote the private interests of their party, at the period of a dissolution of parliament, is not only

only unfair and difingenuous, but is fufficient to awaken the apprehenfion of every man who is either a friend to public peace, or to the prefent happy conftitution.

If indeed we could perceive any thing more of good order, of juftice, or loyalty on the one part, or of meeknefs, charity, or benevolence on the other, likely to refult from the projected reformation, we might fufpect our judgment, and condemn our prejudices. But, on the contrary, we have all the reafon imaginable to conclude, that, fhould thofe fences of the conftitution, thofe bounds betwixt liberty and licentioufnefs, be abolifhed, confequences moft fatal to fociety would enfue. What Solomon fays concerning the "beginning of ftrife," that it is like "the letting out of water," might then be exemplified: for, if thefe flood-gates were once opened, we know not where the inundation would ftop. Whilft one would be cavilling at ordinances, another contending againft the admiffion and authority of fcripture, a third reforming church eftablifhments, and a fourth demolifhing every femblance of epifcopal government, we may well imagine, that the various opinions of the reformers, *now entrufted with executive power*, would create a fpirit of oppofition, not to be confined to argument and reafoning, but that would infenfibly draw in the arm of magiftracy, in order to enforce a compliance with this or that favourite fyftem: and, if the horrors of civil war were not to be apprehended, we fhould certainly fee that fcene of mutual intolerance revived,

vived, which is one object of a regular establishment to suppress.—But to take this reformation in its less frightful point of view. If once these fences, the Tests, are thrown down, and a broad road to Babel is paved by civil authority, the ridicule of atheism, and the triumph of infidelity, would be complete. The unavoidable pollution of the altars of religion, and the distraction that would pervade her temples, whilst one was crying out, " *Ecce in deserto!*" and another, " *Ecce in penetra-* " *libus!*" would not only excite the mirth of the libertine, but would discompose the features of orthodoxy itself. Nor would the state enjoy more tranquillity, or be exposed to less confusion: for, since the legislature is required to grant a repeal of " *every penal statute against religious principles* *," what an encouragement is there for future associations? The gloomy suicide, and bold blasphemer, the lewd sabbath-breaker, and common swearer, may confederate with the rank advocates for bigamy and concubinage, and, pleading an exemption from penal statutes against *their religious principles,* join the *cry for liberty, equal and impartial liberty.*—The confusion in politics would not be less; Jews and Mussulmen, Rabbins and Mufti, with all the untimely births, and miscellaneous spawn of Christianity, now shaped for comptrollers, clerks, and commissaries, would press forward to the various departments of vacant office and prostrate ma-

* Resolution of the Protestant Dissenters of Bolton.

giftracy. The routine of public bufinefs would be impeded, the folemnity of national council invaded, and the attention of government diftracted

> " Diffentientis conditionibus
> " Fœdis."   HORACE.

Whilft the only probable compenfation would be— the dulnefs of a levee relieved by a morrice-dance of fectaries.

F I N I S.

www.ingramcontent.com/pod-product-compliance
Lightning Source LLC
Chambersburg PA
CBHW030404170426
43202CB00010B/1491